D0468814

Confidence

The power to take control and live the life you want

second edition

Rob Yeung

Prentice Hall Life
is an imprint of

Harlow, England • London • New York • Boston • San Francisco • Toronto • Sydney • Singapore • Hong Kong
Tokyo • Seoul • Taipei • New Delhi • Cape Town • Madrid • Mexico City • Amsterdam • Munich • Paris • Milan

PEARSON EDUCATION LIMITED

Edinburgh Gate
Harlow CM20 2JE
Tel: +44 (0)1279 623623
Fax: +44 (0)1279 431059
Website: www.pearsoned.co.uk

First published in Great Britain in 2008
Second edition 2011

Pearson Education is not responsible for the content of third party internet sites.

ISBN: 978-0-273-74258-6

British Library Cataloguing-in-Publication Data
A catalogue record for this book is available from the British Library

Library of Congress Cataloging-in-Publication Data
Yeung, Rob.
  Confidence : the power to take control and live the life you want / Rob Yeung. -- 2nd ed.
      p. cm.
  Includes index.
  ISBN 978-0-273-74258-6 (pbk.)
  1. Self-confidence. I. Title.

  BF575.S39Y48 2011
  155.2--dc22
                                                    2010046056

10 9 8 7 6 5 4 3 2 1
15 14 13 12 11

Typeset in 10/15pt Iowan Old Style BT by Fakenham Photosetting Ltd, Fakenham, Norfolk
Printed and bound by Ashford Colour Press Ltd., Gosport.

Contents

Confidence when you need it 173

About the author

Psychologist and coach Dr Rob Yeung helps people to achieve their goals. He gives motivational speeches at conferences, consults to organisations and coaches individuals on issues ranging from making a successful career change to confident public speaking. Known for his inspiring and informative style, he helps people to make positive changes in their lives and achieve their potential.

As an international speaker, he addresses audiences ranging from business leaders and entrepreneurs to sales people and college students. As an author, he has written over a dozen books which have been translated into many languages around the world including international bestsellers *Personality: How To Unleash Your Hidden Strengths* (Prentice Hall Life) and *The Extra One Percent: How Small Changes Make Exceptional People* (Macmillan). A popular expert on television, he appears on everything from CNN and BBC news to *Big Brother*, and as the presenter of programmes including *How To Get Your Dream Job* for the BBC.

As a director at leadership consulting firm Talentspace, he helps organisations to design assessment centres to identify high performers. He also coaches individuals on issues such as making a career change, starting a business, and becoming more charismatic.

He gained a Ph.D. in psychology from King's College London and is a chartered psychologist and Associate Fellow of the British Psychological Society. And he's a qualified personal trainer and aerobics instructor too.

Visit www.robyeung.com and www.talentspace.co.uk for more information.

Acknowledgements

Thanks to my parents for their unwavering confidence that I can achieve whatever I set my mind to. To my Talentspace colleagues for being there. To Steve Cuthbertson for creating the eye in the sometimes stormy world I inhabit. To Bonnie Chiang and Mandy Wheeler for their comments. To my editor Sam Jackson for her ongoing support. And to the many readers of the first edition who emailed me with comments, this book is ultimately for you.

Preface to the second edition

Confidence, self-esteem, self-belief, a positive self-image – they all amount to the same thing. If you've ever wished you could be more confident, then this book is for you.

I enjoyed writing the first edition of *Confidence*, but I wasn't quite ready for the fantastic reception that I got from it. The book stayed high in the bestseller charts for months and I received many emails from readers telling me how they had used the techniques within the book to boost their confidence and, in some cases, totally overhaul their lives. I received messages telling me about new jobs they had got, new partners they had met, difficult circumstances they'd got over, and so on.

Readers were also kind enough to offer constructive criticism about the book too. I always say to my clients that constructive criticism is a gift. The best thing anyone can do if they don't like you and don't want you to succeed is to say nothing to you. Criticism allows us to identify what's not working or could be better. So this second edition is my attempt to make this not just a very good book, but an excellent one, a book that will hopefully allow many more people to grow in confidence, pursue more opportunities, and ultimately achieve more in their lives.

Based on readers' comments, I've added more advice or guidance around particular exercises. I've also included quite a few brand new techniques and activities that my coaching clients have found particularly useful in the years since I wrote the first edition.

But the biggest changes are in Part 2, which I've expanded considerably. Part 1 provides you with a programme for developing life-long confidence while Part 2 is full of pithy chapters about confidence in specific situations. In the first edition, each of these chapters covered 7 points. I've now expanded each of these chapters to 10 points to give you more guidance.

I've also added new chapters on confident conflict resolution and becoming more confident about your health and body. There's a new chapter on quick confidence if you need a speedy pick-me-up too. And while the first edition of this book had a single chapter on confident socialising and dating, I've separated the two topics into their own chapters because making friends isn't always the same as meeting someone special. If you can think of any more situations in which you'd like to feel more confident, drop me an email! You can reach me through my website www.robyeung.com, or follow me on Twitter @RobYeung.

Confident people have more fun. They earn more, enjoy more fulfilling relationships, and get more out of life. Thankfully, we can all feel more confident and achieve more in our lives if we are prepared to make small changes and invest in ourselves. Let's get started.

Introduction

Want to transform your life and have astounding levels of confidence? The good news is that you can. Because no matter how much or how little confidence you have, you can always have more.

It's a myth that most people are confident. In fact, *many* people report that they would like to feel more confident. People who appear confident on the outside may still feel nervous inside. People who are confident at work may be shy when it comes to dating; people who are confident at parties may feel panicky giving presentations. So if you would like to be more confident, you're in good company.

Confidence is not something that you are born either with or without. Confidence is not an all-or-nothing personality trait that you're stuck with for life. We are all capable of feeling more confident. We can nurture and develop our confidence at any age by adopting new behaviours and strategies. So whether you're 18 or 88, you can learn, grow, and help yourself to achieve your potential. Best of all, you already have all of the resources that you need – my job in writing this book is to help you to discover and develop those resources within yourself.

Perhaps you need more confidence in a particular situation such as speaking in front of an audience or facing up to a colleague, asking someone on a date, taking an exam, or making an impact during interviews. Perhaps you're trying to get over a relationship break-up or worried about the state of the world. Or maybe you crave more confidence in several areas of your life. You may be only mildly worried by certain situations or stricken by self-doubt and paralysing fears. From the boardroom to the bedroom, this book is filled with easy-to-use techniques and exercises for boosting your confidence and helping you to get the best from your life.

This stuff works!

To help you become your best, most confident self, I have packed this book with techniques, tips, and scientifically proven exercises. I have drawn on the best from fields including cognitive behavioural therapy, sport psychology, neuro-linguistic programming, and positive psychology. Some of it is so cutting-edge you could get paper cuts simply turning the pages. Don't worry if that sounds like so much gobbledygook – take it on trust that I qualified as a psychologist and have scoured the worlds of academia, business, and coaching to bring you only stuff that works.

That's because I have been frustrated over the years that there are books on confidence that simply do not deliver results. I'm afraid there are frauds, quacks and self-taught life coaches who tout fluffy, frivolous ideas that do not have a lasting impact on confidence. Sure, some of their techniques may feel good for days or even weeks – but do they deliver long-term benefits? No. Well this book is different.

Take note throughout the book of one-off 'Take Action' exercises, as well as 'Confidence Booster' techniques that you will want to use again and again. Using these, you will learn not only how to project a more confident image but also how to change the way you think and feel about yourself and the world. The result? You will build a profound and lasting confidence to deal with just about anything that life could throw at you. If you put your trust in Dr Rob, I won't let you down.

A personal story

I wholeheartedly believe that confidence can be built. And I speak as both a psychologist and someone who used to suffer from crippling fears. When I was younger, I was so petrified of public speaking to even a handful of people that I felt physically sick – I literally used to retch as if I were going to throw up. I was so scared that I used to pretend I was ill to get out of doing it. But I've since trained myself to love speaking to audiences of many hundreds of people at a time. And as I sometimes appear on TV, on programmes ranging from BBC shows to CNN news and *Big Brother*, I now get the biggest buzz from being in the spotlight on live television in front of millions of people.

But I wouldn't say that I'm anything special. I'm an ordinary person who used to suffer from a lack of confidence but applied some techniques to boost it. My message: if I can do it, so can you.

Get involved

By using this book, you'll learn how to lift your confidence quickly. No matter what your state of mind, I guarantee that investing a few minutes every day on the tools within this book will act like a shot of steroids to your confidence. Almost immediately, you will feel more relaxed and energised. And in the long term you will develop such unassailable levels of jut-jawed confidence that you will be able to handle just about *anything*.

BUT – and here's the but – to get the most out of this book, you can't just read it and set it aside. You have to *do* the exercises and *use* the techniques. This book can transform your levels of confidence and help you to achieve a more satisfying and successful life. But only if you put in the work! A football coach trains and advises a team but ultimately has to trust the players to deliver on the football field. So think of me as your confidence coach. My job is to offer you the latest in scientifically proven techniques and exercises. But you are the one who has to go out on the football pitch of your own life.

Feel free to work through this book at your own pace. Whether you want to race through it all at once, take the journey more leisurely, or flick backwards and forwards between interesting chapters, the choice is yours. But reading and appreciating how the ideas in this book might work for people in general is not the same as applying them in your own life. So make sure you do the fun interactive activities and exercises. You need to do the thinking, put pen to paper, take action.

Understanding the principles is not the same as using them. So each time you come across an exercise, please complete it before you move on. Each time you learn a new technique, find the time to use it in your everyday life. The more you participate with this book, refer to it, scribble your thoughts in the margins, highlight passages that jump out at you, and note techniques you want to try again and again, the more your confidence will swell. Don't just read – get involved.

Life-long confidence *and* immediate needs

I've divided this book into two parts. Part 1 takes you on a journey to build a sense of confidence that will see you through the rest of your life. You will understand how to enhance your confidence, no matter how little of it you currently have. You will work through exercises to open your eyes to untapped strengths and personal resources. You will learn tricks to apply in all sorts of situations, not only to appear more self-assured but also to create a confident mindset.

Part 2 is different because it tackles in greater detail the common situations that many people find daunting. I offer practical advice on 8 specific topics:

- Giving polished presentations and speeches (Chapter 8 on page 175).

- Socialising, meeting new people, and becoming a confident conversationalist (Chapter 9 on page 187).

- Asking people out and confident dating (Chapter 10 on page 197).

- Becoming more effective during meetings at work as well as networking, for example at conferences (Chapter 11 on page 207).

- Performing well at job interviews by preparing well and countering nerves (Chapter 12 on page 215).

- Making change happen in your life, which could include anything from leaving a bad situation to starting your own business (Chapter 13 on page 225).

- Learning to deal with conflict in a firm yet non-confrontational manner (Chapter 14 on page 235).

- Improving your health, fitness and confidence with your body (Chapter 15 on page 245).

I end Part 2 with Chapter 16 on 'Quick confidence' (on page 257). In this final chapter, I provide you with tools and techniques for dealing with worries and bolstering your confidence as quickly as possible. Feel free to flick ahead if one or more of those topics spring out at you!

Time to get started

I would wish you good luck, but you don't need luck. Your fate is within your control. Success depends only on your decision to use the tools within this book. Do the work and you will gain the confidence. It really is that simple. So enjoy the book and drop me an email through my website www.robyeung.com to share your successes with me.

Anyway, are you ready to get going? Let's kick off our journey to craft the new, more confident you.

Dr Rob Yeung

Part 1

Developing life-long confidence

01

Confidence and you

"What the mind can conceive, the mind can achieve."
Clement Stone, entrepreneur and philanthropist

In this chapter you will ...

- learn what confidence is and what it can allow you to achieve
- understand that you can take control of your life, no matter what's going on around you right now
- discover how your thoughts and behaviour influence how you feel about yourself
- measure your current levels of confidence and uncover the areas of your life that most need changing.

So what comes to mind when we talk about confidence? Perhaps you think of confidence as how people behave. Think of the confident folks you know and maybe you imagine how they laugh and smile, give unwavering presentations or seem to ace job interviews. Or you see them mingling with strangers, acting larger-than-life, and happily being the centre of attention.

But how people come across is only a part of being confident. Most of what makes up confidence is what confidence allows you to *achieve*. Because there are people who are quietly confident – who don't draw attention to themselves but manage to conquer life's challenges and get what they want from life.

And that's what confidence is mainly about – allowing people to achieve their goals. Because confident people:

- grasp new opportunities
- cope with setbacks and bounce back from rejection
- deal with new situations, difficulties and opportunities – seeing them as challenges to be tackled and overcome rather than threats to be avoided
- take responsibility for making change happen rather than wishing their circumstances or the people around them would change
- may feel anxiety, worry, and fear but push on regardless in order to achieve their long-term goals

■ have a sense of purpose and set both long- and short-term goals to pursue what they want from life.

Interested? Does any of that sound appealing?

As you can see from the list, confidence is not always about feeling good inside. Yes, confident people can feel self-assured and good about themselves. But they sometimes feel scared or overwhelmed too. Confident people can still feel anxious about important projects at work or troubles in their personal lives. The difference between confident people and less confident people is not in how much they *feel* fear or anxiety, but in how confident people put up with those feelings and deal with their situations regardless.

OK, so that's what confidence allows people – and that includes you – to do. But what is confidence exactly? And how can you get more of it?

Confidence is about action

Let's define confidence. I say that confidence is 'the ability to take appropriate and effective action, however challenging it may feel at the time'. Confidence isn't the absence of fear; it's about taking action *in spite* of how we may feel, in the knowledge that action will eventually help us to conquer how we feel. Confidence is about doing what you need to do in the short term to achieve your long-term goals, even if what you need to do in the short term may feel temporarily uncomfortable.

Sure, you may feel daunted by a task or situation. But becoming confident is about learning to manage those feelings in order to achieve your long-term goals. Say you're worried about taking an exam or going for a job interview; you will do it anyway because your goal is to succeed in life. If you're anxious about speaking in public, you will grit your teeth and do it because it will further your career. If you shy away from meeting new people, coping with rejection, asserting yourself, beginning or ending relationships, or whatever else it may be, you will train yourself to do so because it will enhance your long-term happiness.

If you ever feel nervous, you're not alone. In fact, you're in very good company. I think it's safe to assume that *most* people sometimes feel nervous or even outright scared by the tasks they have to do. The secret is not to let your feelings stop you from doing anything, but to do it anyway.

A little bit of nervousness can even be healthy. Feeling nervous ensures that we don't become arrogant or complacent. It's our brain's way of telling us that we mustn't let our guard down or take anything for granted. We need to perk up, pay attention, and make an effort to ensure that we can be at our best.

You'd be surprised how many people still get anxious. They may *appear* confident, but they may still be wracked with the same feelings of nerves and insecurity as the rest of us. In a recent interview, legendary singer Dame Shirley Bassey admitted: 'I get more nervous now about going on stage than I ever did.' But that hasn't stopped her from performing to thousands of people at concerts or even millions on live television.

I once coached an international rugby player – one of the England team who won the Rugby World Cup in 2003. Known for being super-cool on the pitch, he was worried about standing up and giving speeches to even smallish groups of business people. But despite his nerves, he was determined to become a successful public speaker.

And you know what? The more you throw yourself into situations that scare you, the more likely you are to enjoy them. At some point, you will forget that you're scared and actually start to feel exhilarated, alive, and liberated by what you're doing.

I used to be scared of speaking in public. But with practice I overcame my fears. I stopped being scared and I started to love public speaking.

So the lesson is this: the feeling of confidence comes *after* action, not before it.

"Courage is resistance to fear, mastery of fear – not absence of fear."

Mark Twain, writer

Over to you

What made you pick this book up? If confidence is about action, start by scribbling your aims on a sheet of paper or even in the margin of this book. Write a couple of sentences that capture what you'd like to get out of this book: in what ways would you like to be more confident? To get you started, here's a list of common situations in which many people feel they could be more confident.

Taking a driving test

Asking someone out on a date

Pursuing opportunities and taking risks

Handling criticism

Learning a new skill

Beginning or ending a relationship

Dealing with colleagues or customers

Impressing at job interviews

Leaving a bad situation

Networking at conferences

Recovering from a trauma

Losing weight or getting fitter

Being more assertive

Speaking in public

Changing career

Making new friends

Coping with rejection

Asking for a pay rise

Changing your life

Taking an exam or test

Receiving compliments

Being a parent

Learning to say 'no' to people

Overcoming fears or worries

Take action

I want to get across a key message right now: confidence is about taking action, taking control. A lot of people who want more confidence *wish* that their lives would change. They wish their boss were more helpful, their spouse more caring. They wish they had more time or money. They wish they had done something differently in the past or that someone would give them the chance.

But unless you have a reliable genie or a fairy godmother on call, wishing is not a strategy. Your boss is unlikely to become more helpful spontaneously – you either need to work around them or find a different job with a more helpful boss. If you don't have enough time or money (and who does, these days?), then it's up to you to free up a bit more time or set aside a bit of extra cash. If you don't make it happen, it ain't gonna happen by itself.

I beg you: please don't play the wishing game! If you've been wishing, waiting, hoping in the past, that's fine. But seize the moment now. Rather than waiting any longer for your circumstances to change and grant you more confidence, why not go out and grab it?

I'm sure you have heard of people who triumphed over severe adversity. People who suffered extreme poverty, cruelty and abuse, physical disability or crippling illness, and still managed to overcome their difficulties and succeed. They could have wallowed in their misfortunes and complained 'If only my parents hadn't neglected me' or 'If only I hadn't been struck down with cancer'. But they didn't. And the message to take from them is that you *can* succeed no matter what your circumstances. Many people have gruelling backgrounds but still manage to elevate themselves from them. And if *you* want to improve and grow, you can. Be captain of your own destiny. Simply decide to take action.

Think about your situation for a moment. What constraints are holding you back right now? Perhaps a lack of time, a difficult situation at home, or an uncaring boss? A tough childhood, a lack of the right qualifications, or an unsupportive family? Not enough money, a bout of ill-health or a lack of fitness? Rather than seeing these as insurmountable barriers stopping you from becoming more confident, you can see them as challenges to be overcome. And, in this book, I'll show you how.

Over to you

There's a saying that the road to hell is paved with good intentions. No matter how good our intentions, we sometimes don't get round to taking action. Thankfully, psychologists have discovered a principle known as congruence. When we make a commitment (even if that commitment is only to ourselves), we don't like to make liars of ourselves so we are more likely to behave in ways that are congruent with our commitments. So making even a small commitment can boost our chances of successfully turning our intentions into actions.

If you want to give yourself the best shot at actually increasing your confidence and achieving more with your life, then read and sign this contract. It's a promise to yourself. Feel free to type it out or write it out. You can even reword it if you want to make it even more specific to you.

I .. RYAN HARRIS promise not only to read this book but actually pick up pen and paper to try out some of the exercises and techniques. I will do this because I want to feel more confident and get more out of life.

Signed .. Ryan Harris

Congratulations. You've taken the first step for yourself. That wasn't too difficult, was it?

"Every man is the architect of his own fortune."

Proverb

9

Being scared can't kill you

Of course you may be scared at the thought of having to tackle your fears head-on. However, bear in mind that feelings are not reality. Your worries may loom larger than life and cause you a lot of grief – but your worries are only a trick played on you by your own mind. Feeling worried, anxious, scared, sad, or whatever else you may feel, won't kill you. We are lucky in the modern world that most of the things that frighten us aren't actually fatal. In fact, the worst that can happen is rarely as bad as your imagination suggests.

Over to you

Think about your own experience:

- What's the scariest thing you have ever done?

- How did it turn out?

You might have been really worried in the run-up to an exam, a talk, or a crucial meeting. Maybe you did something knee-tremblingly terrifying such as a bungee jump for charity. You may have suffered sleepless nights beforehand and incredible nerves on the big day. But how did it go? Probably much better than you thought it would. And the fact that you're reading this book means that you lived to tell the tale!

The cycle of confidence

OK, we've established that confidence is about taking action and taking control. But what exactly are you taking control of? The answer: what you *do*, *think*, and *feel*.

Psychologists have known for a long time that what you *feel*, *do*, and *think* are linked in a cycle, a continuous loop. Suppose someone *feels* nervous about going to a party on her own. So what she *does* is stay at home. Which makes her *think* that she

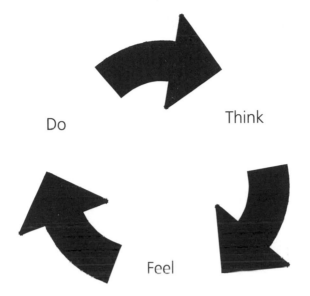

Do   Think

Feel

will be lonely for ever, making her *feel* unhappy and even less confident about future parties.

Or someone *thinks* he is a loser. By thinking he's a loser, he *feels* unhappy, making him even less likely to *do* anything. He can't muster up the energy to try new things and ends up proving himself right that he's a loser.

If you let your feelings get the better of you, you create a vicious cycle, a self-perpetuating loop that reinforces your fears and drains your confidence.

On the other hand, if you *think* differently, you *feel* differently, and *do* differently. Force yourself to *think* more positively and you start to *feel* happy and confident. Which gives you the kick you need to *do* something new, which in turn reinforces your positive thinking and feelings. And so it goes round again, creating a virtuous cycle that grows your confidence.

The absolutely fantastic news is that you can develop your confidence by intervening at any of the three stages. For example, let's start with the doing. If you behave ('do') as if you are already confident – going to that party, giving a presentation at work, asking someone out on a date – you make it easier for yourself to believe ('think') that you can be confident. In turn, thinking more positively helps you to be ('feel') more relaxed and confident, which helps you to do even more. If you follow the steps in this book by changing your behaviour and ways of thinking, the confidence will come.

Assessing where you are now

Before we look at how to change, let's look at what needs changing. How confident do you feel at the moment?

Read through the following statements and decide how much you agree with each one. Bear in mind that this quiz is for your own use, so be honest. If you score yourself higher than you really feel, you only kid yourself. To work out your score on the self-confidence scale, use the following scoring guide:

1	2	3	4	5
'disagree strongly'	'disagree slightly'	'neither agree nor disagree'	'agree slightly'	'agree strongly'

The Self-Confidence Scale

Statement	1	2	3	4	5
I always manage to solve difficult problems if I try hard enough.				✓	
If people oppose me, I can find ways to achieve what I want.				✓	
I find it easy to stick to my aims and achieve my goals.				✓	
I am resourceful enough to handle unforeseen situations in all of the different areas of my life.		✓			

Statement	1	2	3	4	5
I am confident that I can deal effectively with unexpected events and setbacks.	✓				
I usually say 'yes' to new opportunities.		✓			
I remain calm when faced with difficulties in both my personal and professional life.	✓				
I can solve most of the problems I am confronted with.			✓		
I feel passionate, fulfilled and alive most of the time.			✓		
I am certain that I can handle whatever comes my way.	✓				

Understanding your rating

Now add up your scores from the 10 statements to get an overall score between 10 and 50. What does your score say about you?

- **Score of between 41 and 50:** You are a confident person who believes firmly in your abilities to overcome difficulties, solve problems, and succeed even in the face of adversity. Scan through the book and choose the handful of Take Action exercises and Confidence Booster techniques that will help you to maintain your high levels of confidence.

- **Score of between 31 and 40:** You are confident most of the time in your ability to deal with the situations and impasses that you encounter. Like most people, you may be more confident in some areas of your life than others. Work through the Take Action exercises and explore which of the Confidence Boosters could help you to improve your confidence just that little bit more.

- **Score of between 21 and 30:** Your confidence could be somewhat higher. Perhaps you are feeling a little anxious or experiencing some uncertainty about how to deal with your circumstances. But using the Confidence Boosters and Take

Action exercises will help you to develop both day-to-day and longer-term confidence.

■ **Score of between 10 and 20**: Your confidence seems to be rather low at the moment, but we can work on that. In fact, the lower your confidence, the easier it is to make quick progress. Start with the Confidence Boosters in Chapter 2 to change your beliefs, your view of life. But don't take too much on at once – make sure you become familiar with each technique and have incorporated it into your life before you move on to the next one.

Once you have totalled up your score, take a note of it right now. Maybe jot your score in the margin of this book along with today's date. Irrespective of your score today, you will see your confidence grow as you use the tools in this book. Come back to complete the test again in six months' time and you are certain to record a much higher score.

Eight spheres of a confident life

Most of us live at such a furious pace that we don't get the chance to ask ourselves how we're doing and what we want from life. Well this is your chance now.

The questionnaire you just completed looks at how much confidence you have at the moment. And I know I've already asked you to think of certain situations that you would like to have more confidence in. But sometimes people need confidence in ways that are to do less with specific situations and more with broader areas of their lives. And that's what this next exercise sets out to measure.

Look at the eight spheres of a confident life and score your level of confidence in each on a scale of 1 to 10. A '10' represents incredibly high levels of confidence – you are not only totally satisfied with how you feel in this area of your life, but other people probably look on in astonishment at what you have achieved in it too. A '1' score represents very low levels of confidence – you urgently want to change what's happening within this area of your life.

Remember that, as with all of the exercises in this book, the results are for you alone. No one else sees them, so be honest in how you rate the different areas of your life. Put a tick in each box to represent your satisfaction with each area.

Scoring the eight spheres of a confident life

	1	2	3	4	5	6	7	8	9	10
Your physical life						✓				
Your intimate life						✓				
Your family life			✓							
Your social life					✓					
Your occupational life							✓			
Your financial life					✓					
Your sense of purpose in life		✓								
Your fun life					✓					

The eight spheres of a confident life are as follows:

■ **Your physical life**. Consider your confidence in your physical health, fitness, diet, energy levels, and well-being. Are you concerned with your health? Do you feel strong and healthy all of the time or do you have aches and pains, coughs and colds? A '10' score implies you're someone who springs out of bed in the mornings with boundless energy, confident in the knowledge that you will be able to take on anything during the course of the day and still have the energy to do more during the evening until you decide to go to bed. A lower score implies you often feel tired, ill, or that you could look after yourself better.

■ **Your intimate life**. Think about your level of confidence in your relationship with your partner, spouse, or significant other. Think about your partner right now: does your partner support you, make you laugh and feel loved, bring you joy and happiness? A high level of confidence means that you are deeply satisfied with your relationship. Or, if you do not have a partner, you may still score this area highly if you are completely happy as an independent person. A low score means that you could feel a lot happier – either because you wish you could improve the quality of your existing relationship or because you yearn to be with someone.

■ **Your family life**. Think about your relationships with your parents, any siblings, children, and your wider network of family and relatives. Do you feel totally loved and supported by your family? Consider the extent to which you feel confident enough to be yourself with them. How confident do you generally feel when dealing with your family and asking them for what you need?

■ **Your social life**. How confident do you feel about your social life? Do you see your friends as much as you would like? Do they get in touch with you often enough? Do you have the confidence to meet new people and make new friends? A high score implies that your social life exceeds your expectations. A low score may mean that you would like to be more confident in your relationships with your friends.

■ **Your work life**. Consider how confident you feel at work. To what extent do you feel fulfilled and thrilled by your work? Do you feel confident that your work allows you to express the person you want to be? A high score implies that you are happy with the nature of your work, your prospects, and the relationships you have at work. However, if you consider your work to be a chore that you do only to pay the bills, you may wish to score this area lower.

- **Your financial life.** Consider your confidence in your ability to *manage* your money. How confident are you that you are able to provide for yourself and your loved ones? That you are able to pay the bills and put something aside? Most of us could easily do with a little more money, but this sphere is not about how much money you have. Some people earn millions but still worry about having enough. Others earn very little and yet live contentedly within their means. How much confidence do you have in your ability to manage your finances and feel secure with the money you have?

- **Your sense of purpose in life.** Confident people have a sense of purpose and meaning in their lives. They feel confident that they have tasks to perform in their time on Earth – they give freely of their time, energy, and other resources without expectation of anything in return. Others lack that confidence and certainty, drifting from one day to the next. People who score highly on this sphere often get involved with causes such as community groups, charities, their faith or religion, society, the environment, and so on. In what ways do you contribute to the wider world? How confident are you that you live a meaningful life?

- **Your fun life.** Not everything in life is about serving causes or other people. We need to take time for ourselves, to have fun, to be creative, to do activities that we enjoy doing simply for their own sake. Otherwise life can feel like hard work, a series of never-ending chores that have to be done. Having fun at least occasionally allows us to recharge our batteries and help us to retain a balanced perspective on life. To what extent are you able to engage in pleasurable hobbies or enthralling activities that allow you to feel good about yourself?

I have left two lines of the table blank for you to add any further areas of your life that are important to you. For example, some people crave recognition for their efforts or have a faith that they wish to follow. You are unique and may have your own areas that you need to pay attention to in order to feel satisfied and fulfilled in your whole life. So before you read on, consider: what else might be really essential to you in your life and need capturing in the table on page 15?

When you've scored the eight spheres of your life, give yourself a pat on the back. So many people live their lives feeling anything from slightly dissatisfied to downright miserable and yet do nothing about it. But not you. By rating the level of confidence you have in the different areas of your life, you are putting a stake in the ground, making a commitment to yourself, and giving yourself a good shot at changing your prospects.

Once you've put your ticks in the different boxes, consider *why* you've given yourself these scores. Give each sphere a little thought. Write a few notes on what is going on in that sphere of your life. For each sphere, use the following questions to prompt your thinking:

- What is *good* that is currently happening?
- What is *bad* and could do with changing?
- What is *new* that you would like to develop?

If they can do it ...

Alison is a 31-year-old supervisor at an insurance company. She works long hours and feels constantly drained – her first waking thoughts are often of work and she returns every evening with work still spinning in her head. Feeling that her life is slipping away, she reviews the eight spheres of her life. She gives herself high scores in her occupational and financial life and is reasonably content with some of the other areas of her life. She gives herself the lowest scores – 3 out of 10 in both cases – on her intimate life and sense of purpose in life.

She writes a paragraph on each of the spheres, including the following on the two that she scores lowest in.

- **In my intimate life:** I have plenty of friends, but I don't have a relationship in my life. I have plenty of single women friends, so the pressure doesn't feel on to find a partner. But I am sometimes lonely. I'm so busy at work – but do I use my work as an excuse not to meet someone? I have friends who have tried internet dating but I'm too embarrassed to give it a go – I don't want anyone to feel that I'm desperate. On the other hand, I haven't made much progress in recent years. And the fact that I've scored this sphere as a 3 must mean that it's more important to me than I let on even to myself.

- **My sense of purpose in life:** What is my purpose in life? I do think that I'd love to do something for a charity. Whenever I see that advert for the children's charity on TV, I get all these ideas into my head. But then the daily grind of projects at work brings me back down to earth so quickly. I know no one on their deathbed ever wishes they'd spent more time in the office. But what do I really want to do? I'm not sure. I've never had the time – or perhaps more accurately I've never made the time – but maybe I need to find out.

Having invested the time in reviewing the different spheres of her life, Alison commits to giving these two key areas more thought. She picks out a Saturday later in the month and is determined to work through some more exercises and activities then.

You can write as little or as much as you like about the different spheres of your life. Some people find that a few bullet points are enough; other people write a few paragraphs on certain spheres, but pages on other spheres. Do what works for you.

We're going to leave this exercise for now. But we'll come back to it later on in Chapter 4 when we come to putting together a vision for your new, more confident life.

Get ready to succeed

Invest in a good quality notebook, journal or binder that you will be proud to use. You can write your thoughts in it and keep track of your progress as you work through the exercises in this book. By keeping all your reflections in one place, you can refer to them easily in future. And when you come to look back on them, you will quickly be able to see how much progress you have made.

Understanding your sources of confidence

People may have low confidence for all sorts of reasons – their childhood, their genes, their age, their circumstances. But irrespective of what has happened to you in the past and what is happening to you now, you can influence your future. Building your confidence is like assembling the pieces of a jigsaw. Below are the six pieces of the confidence jigsaw that you will pull together in Part 1 of this book.

- **Your mindset and beliefs.** Confident people have positive beliefs and are optimistic about the situations they encounter. But many people beat themselves up for their mistakes and failings or allow their fears and worries to overwhelm them. Thankfully, psychologists have discovered that people can change the way they think. You can train your mind to develop positive, constructive beliefs and a rugged sense of confidence. I tackle how to do this in Chapter 2.

- **Your behaviour.** The *do, think, feel* cycle (on page 11) tells us that if you behave confidently, you can help yourself to think more confidently and feel more confident about yourself. I share with you tips and techniques for behaving in ways that will not only make you *appear* more confident but will also make you *feel* more confident. I cover how to do this in Chapter 3.

- **Your goals**. Confident people have goals – they know what they want to achieve in life. They know when to work hard and when to conserve their energies to achieve their goals. People who don't have goals tend to drift in their lives and allow their circumstances to dent their confidence. I share with you how to identify your goals in Chapter 4.

- **Your resources**. Confident people draw upon all manner of resources in developing and maintaining their confidence. They draw upon the support of other people, their environment, and rituals to feel good about themselves. I tell you how to make the most of your resources in Chapter 5.

- **Your resilience**. Confident people bounce back from setbacks and rejection, adversity and criticism. Even if you can't always control everything that happens to you, you can always control how you choose to respond. I talk about how to recover quickly from setbacks in Chapter 6.

- **Your ways to keep going**. Growing your confidence is a marathon, not a sprint. In Chapter 7 I share with you how to review your progress, keep your motivation high, and make confidence a life-long habit.

Feel free to skip ahead to the chapters that most interest you. If, say, you need to behave confidently immediately, then head to Chapter 3. If you want to find out about using your resources, then Chapter 5 is the one for you. Or if you would like to come with me on the route that we would take if I were coaching you personally towards a more confident you, then let's work through the chapters in order. But before we move on to Chapter 2, congratulate yourself for completing Chapter 1 – your journey to the new you is well on its way.

CONFIDENCE

ONWARDS AND UPWARDS

■ Remember that confidence is the ability to take action, however challenging it may feel at the time. That may mean feeling a bit scared or anxious but deciding to take action anyway in the knowledge that it will get a heck of a lot easier the next time.

■ Confidence is a quality that *anyone* can get more of. Irrespective of your upbringing or education, or whatever constraints are currently holding you back, you can decide to take practical steps to improve your life and renew your confidence.

■ Remember that feeling worried, anxious, frightened, sad, or scared can't kill you! If your confidence is at a low ebb, you must remember that what you are feeling is only your mind playing tricks on you.

■ Remember the *do, think, feel* cycle. If you *do* confidence and *think* confidently, you will quickly *feel* more confident too.

You may currently lack confidence in only specific situations or in quite broad areas of your life. But it doesn't matter what your current circumstances are. By understanding where you are now, together we can work on getting you where you want to go.

02

Developing bullet-proof beliefs

"For they conquer who believe they can."

John Dryden, poet

In this chapter you will ...

■ learn that, while your beliefs have a strong effect on how you feel and behave, they may not always be an accurate reflection of what is going on around you

■ come to appreciate that your beliefs and attitude are not permanent – you can choose to change them

■ discover tried-and-tested techniques for challenging unhelpful beliefs and replacing them with more helpful ones

■ learn to feel motivated and confident by changing the messages you tell yourself and the images you play out in your head

■ explore a simple yet proven method for developing your sense of optimism.

Confidence is a mind game. Confidence comes not from being tall or short, a man or a woman, young or old, or any other physical characteristic. Confident people believe in themselves. And because they believe, they achieve.

Take a moment to ask yourself what you believe about yourself. What messages do you generally feed yourself? Do you mainly tell yourself how strong, talented, and confident you are? Or do you lay into yourself about your mistakes, your weaknesses, and your failings?

Whatever your current state of mind, you can quickly improve your confidence by consciously changing how you think about yourself and the world. By using tried-and-tested techniques, you can think more positively, optimistically, and constructively. You can learn to think confidently in the same way that you can learn to ride a bike or play tennis.

Your thoughts matter

The beliefs you hold and the thoughts you have can mak
you feel strong and excited or tense and unhappy. Some of
these beliefs may be long-held and deep-seated, while other
messages you tell yourself may be more fleeting but no less
damaging to your self-confidence. Tell yourself 'Everyone's
going to laugh at me' or 'I'm going to fail' and your self-confidence withers.

"If you think you can or you think you can't – you're
right."

Henry Ford, car manufacturer

Remember the *do, think, feel* cycle from Chapter 1. If you think
that you are capable of achieving more, you feel positive and
you become able to do more. If you tell yourself (think) you're a
failure, you feel down and ensure you become a failure. Decades
of research back me up on this too: you are what you think.

If you've heard of the placebo effect, you know that belief alone
can heal the human body. Doctors know that giving a dummy
pill with no medicine in it can cure patients with conditions
ranging from angina and asthma to headaches and intestinal
ulcers. Even when patients unknowingly take empty pill cap-
sules or swallow sugar tablets, their belief that they will get
better actually affects their physiologies.

Beliefs are not reality

You are not born with your beliefs, your attitude, your ways of
thinking. Your beliefs are influenced not only by what goes on
around you but also by what you *choose* to believe.

le experiencing exactly the same event can end
t beliefs. Even though the situation may be the
ghts can go in wildly different directions.

on in which six people go for a job interview.
viewed by the managing director, the boss of
business. Unfortunately the boss comes across as cold and
unfriendly during the interview. A few days later they all get a
letter in the post saying 'It was a pleasure to meet you but I'm
afraid that you were not successful in getting the job'. Each
person might explain the reason for being rejected in a different
way. And because of the *do, think, feel* cycle, how they think
about the rejection affects their feelings too. Let's look at the
six different ways each person thinks and feels.

- Person 1 thinks: 'I'm rubbish at interviews – I should never have
  gone for this interview.' They feel depressed.

- Person 2 thinks: 'I wouldn't want to work for that company
  anyway because the boss was so rude!' They feel relieved.

- Person 3 thinks: 'That was a good opportunity for me to
  practise my interview skills. I will continue to go to interviews
  and improve each time until I get a job.' This person feels
  happy.

- Person 4 thinks: 'The interviewer must have hated me.' They
  feel ashamed.

- Person 5 thinks: 'There must have been another candidate with
  better experience'. They feel mildly disappointed.

- Person 6 thinks: 'The managing director's letter says that "it was
  a pleasure" to meet me.' This person feels upbeat and more
  determined to succeed at the next interview.

Six people, one event. Each person experiences the same situation. The facts for each person are the same. But each person
manages to interpret the situation in a different way, leading to
a range of different emotions. Some of the emotions damage

their confidence; other emotions have little effect or even enhance their confidence.

You must understand: your beliefs are not the same as reality. Yes they *feel* real, but they are only your interpretation, *one* perspective, on what's going on. Even though you may hold strong beliefs about yourself and your abilities, your beliefs exist because of the way you think – and not because the world is that way.

The voice within

"When you doubt your power, you give power to your doubt."

Anonymous

Imagine for a moment that you have a house guest who keeps telling you how rubbish and stupid you are. From the first thing in the morning, your house guest tells you how foolish you are to consider doing anything new like inviting an attractive person out on a date, asking your boss for a raise, or looking for a new job. Imagine that your guest keeps putting you down all day long, telling you what's wrong with you dozens and dozens of times. And before you fall asleep, your guest reminds you of all the mistakes you've made so that you can relive them all over again.

How would that make you feel? Of course, putting up with someone like that in your life would grate on your nerves and make you miserable. But that's exactly what many of us have. A guest – not in our house – but in our head who condemns us and makes us feel bad.

We all have an inner voice – experts call it our self-talk. You're probably hearing it right now as you read this sentence. Say hello to your inner voice. Hello!

Your inner voice may speak to you in the first person (e.g. 'I'm really bored right now') or the second person (e.g. 'You need to water the plants before you go on holiday') or switch back and forth between the two. It acts as a running commentary on what you're doing, what you've done, and what you need to be doing. This can be useful in reminding you of stuff you have to do, such as 'The weather forecast said it was going to rain today – I should take an umbrella with me' or 'Remember to get a birthday card for Sarah before the weekend'. But the voice inside your head can also compliment or criticise you. And if you're like most people, you probably don't hear your inner voice making positive comments too often. The voice is more likely to be acting as an inner critic, saying 'That looks really scary', 'Everyone's looking at me', or 'I'm going to fail and look stupid if I give this a go so I'd better not bother trying'.

Experts estimate that we say between 150 and 300 words a minute when we engage in this internal banter. As you can imagine, this can add up to thousands of internal messages every day. Unsurprisingly, your inner critic influences the way you see the world, filtering your experience and shaping your beliefs. It acts as a far harsher judge of you than anyone else could ever be.

If you're not feeling as confident as you could be, your inner critic is probably shooting down your ideas and blaming you for your mistakes. Let's help you to kick out your inner critic and replace it with an inner coach instead.

Over to you

Consider:

- What messages do you tend to tell yourself?
- Are they mostly positive or negative?
- What kind of messages would you prefer to feed yourself?

Creeping in our heads

You probably don't spend a lot of time thinking about the way you think. After all, you've been doing it for as long as you can remember. It just happens, it's automatic. But that can be dangerous. Because negative thoughts can pop into your head from your subconscious without you consciously asking for them. And the more you tell yourself that you're a failure or stupid or whatever else you criticise yourself for, the stronger your beliefs become. And because of the *do, think, feel* cycle, when you think yourself to be stupid or ridiculous or a failure, you start to feel and behave that way to prove yourself right.

Psychologists call the unbidden criticisms that pop into our heads *automatic negative thoughts* (ANTs). They can take many forms, but here are a few examples:

- 'I can't do it – I'm not bright enough to succeed.'
- 'People just don't like me.'
- 'I'll never change – I'm too old and set in my ways.'
- 'Everyone will laugh at me if I mess this up.'
- 'It's too difficult.'

You can rest assured that nearly everyone falls prey to occasional ANTs. Even Olympic athletes and top-flight sports people experience doubts and worries. World-class competitors in tennis, golf, swimming and other disciplines recognise that their physical prowess must be matched by a positive internal dialogue.

And that's what you are going to learn to do. Over four decades of research and practice tell us that you can consciously monitor your thoughts, spot the ANTs for the little monsters that they are, and exterminate them from your head.

Get ready to succeed

Your beliefs have probably developed over the years as a result of your upbringing, religion, culture, personal circumstances, and so on. But you may be pleased to hear that you don't have to worry about where they come from! Twenty-first century psychology tells us that you don't have to dig up the past, dredge up unhappy memories, or revisit old feelings. What happened in your past can stay in the past. To be happier and more confident, you need only live in the present and tackle the thoughts that are bothering you now.

"The greatest discovery of my generation is that people can alter their lives by altering their attitudes of mind."

William James, philosopher

Rallying behind your inner coach

Your inner critic can be a pain in the neck. Take on a new challenge and it whispers: 'This will go horribly wrong', 'You're a fool to expose yourself like this', 'You'll be sorry!' But you can drown it out.

This first Confidence Booster summons forth your inner coach. Perhaps you're getting ready to give a presentation, struggling with a difficult problem, or trying to motivate yourself to do 10 more minutes at the gym. In mere minutes you can arm yourself with a handful of capability-affirming thoughts (CATs) to replace your automatic negative thoughts (ANTs).

Confidence Booster: Creating your cool CATs

CATs are capability-affirming thoughts. You may have heard people call them positive affirmations or helpful self-talk. Take a moment to jot down constructive statements you could say to yourself when your confidence is threatened. Consider different CATs for different situations. What you tell yourself just before your big speech may differ from what you say when you're trying to motivate yourself to do an extra 10 minutes on the treadmill or when you're struggling with a thorny problem at your desk. Imagine your very own coach standing next to you, rallying you on, motivating you to keep going, encouraging you to be the best you can. Examples include:

- 'Come on, you can do it!'

- 'I'm determined to get this done.'

- 'Keep smiling.'

- 'I'm much tougher than people think.'

- 'Think of the benefits when you finish!'

- 'Stay confident.'

- 'I've done this before – I can do it again!'

Memorise your CATs or jot them on a sheet of card to keep at hand. Then repeat your CATs to yourself whenever you need a lift. Verbalise them out loud with strength and certainty. Or go over them silently in your head if you could be overheard.

Need convincing that CATs work? Psychologist Michael Mahoney, then at Pennsylvania State University, studied a group of gymnasts hoping to qualify for the US Olympic team. He asked the gymnasts to talk about their thoughts during competitions. He found that the most successful athletes – those who qualified for the Olympic team – had as many doubts and worries as the less successful ones.

If they can do it ...

Nick is a 38-year-old human resources manager who has always considered his strength to be with people rather than numbers. However, he has been asked by his boss to perform some in-depth analyses of the organisation's employee absenteeism and retention data. He feels he can't turn the request down without damaging his career credibility. So, despite believing that he isn't very good with numbers, he has to give it a go.

To assist him on his way, he jots down several capability-affirming thoughts (CATs) to repeat back to himself as he slogs through the task. He picks the four that seem most appropriate to the task ahead:

- 'I can do it.'

- 'I can do anything I set my mind to.'

- 'I'm better than I give myself credit for.'

- 'Keep concentrating.'

Working on the task, he repeats the statements to himself – both silently in his head and quietly out loud if no one is in earshot. He finds that he is able to quell the anxiety he feels about having to work on the analytical problem. Plus he makes progress on it more quickly than he expected. He comes out of it feeling that he can handle whatever his job can throw at him – even those dreaded numbers.

However, the successful athletes constantly encouraged themselves by engaging in more positive self-talk. Tell yourself that you can do it and you go a long way towards proving yourself right.

I use CATs when I'm at my computer and feeling overloaded with work, with reports to write, invoices to send to clients, and more paperwork than I feel I can cope with. To ensure you get the best effect, choose CATs that are meaningful to you and your situation. What you say to yourself when you want to be a gracious guest at a cocktail party may differ from what you tell yourself when you're grappling with a tough problem at work.

Over to you

Can you think of a situation that's coming up in which you'd like to feel more confident? It could be at work or outside of it, in a situation where you're on your own or surrounded by people. What helpful CAT statements could you repeat to yourself? Write them down here.

■ ....

■ ....

■ ....

■ ....

Combating persistent doubts

We've talked about automatic negative thoughts that pop up from time to time. But sometimes we may hear the same negative thoughts again and again. If automatic negative thoughts are ANTs, then these more persistent negative thoughts are just NTs. Maybe an unhelpful teacher or a critical grown-up once said something to you in your childhood and it stuck. A boss, ex-colleague or just an ex criticised you and you took it to heart. Or maybe you didn't do well at something early on in life and blamed yourself for not having been good enough. Any of these sound familiar?

■ 'I'm not clever enough.'

■ 'I've always been rubbish at ...'

■ 'I'm just no good at maths/languages/computers/relationships/ sport.'

■ 'I'm just unlucky that way.'

■ 'I'm too stupid/ugly/short/fat to ...'

■ 'I'll never be any good at ...'

As I'm sure you appreciate by now, negative thoughts can hold us back; they not only make us feel less-than-confident but also stop us from achieving our potential. Thankfully, we can take stock of unhelpful beliefs and replace them with more useful ones.

Take Action: Doing a CAT scan

In medicine, a CAT (Computerised Axial Tomography) scan is a type of X-ray procedure used by doctors to identify injuries or health problems. But in the context of our confidence, a CAT scan is a way of detecting enduring negative thoughts and replacing them with capability-affirming thoughts (CATs).

Over the course of the next few weeks, keep a record of the persistent negative beliefs you hold about yourself. Write these down either as soon after you experience them as you can or perhaps at the end of every day.

Every time you spot a new negative thought, write out a new, more constructive capability-affirming thought (CAT) to replace it. The key, however, is to focus on how your actions and efforts are helping you to improve. So good examples of CATs include:

■ 'My skill at this grows every time I try it.'

■ 'I can achieve more when I work hard at this.'

■ 'I am making an effort to get better at …'

■ 'I am improving on this with every minute I spend on it.'

■ 'I'm better at this now than I was last week/month/year.'

■ 'I am making progress because of the time and effort I am investing in this.'

Whenever you find yourself dwelling on any of your persistent negative thoughts, simply bring to mind one of your new CATs. Over time, you will retrain the way you speak to yourself and find your confidence lifting.

I'm not recommending that you try to trick your mind by making overblown claims such as 'I am a beautiful person', 'I am brilliant and amazing' or 'I am clever and capable'. No, those kinds of statements are more like wishful thinking; you yourself probably won't believe such fanciful claims. To be effective, you have to create CATs that are plausible; they have to be grounded in reality and based on the actual actions you're taking, the practice you're putting in, the effort you're making, and so on.

Vanquishing your mental monsters

The CAT Confidence Booster and CAT scan are great ways to start rooting out your ANTs. But if the CAT is like a pistol for picking off ANTs, this next Confidence Booster is the big gun, your mega-missile, for blowing those ANTs away entirely.

Sometimes you may feel so emotionally overwrought, your thoughts and feelings so tightly intertwined, that it's difficult to think clearly at all. Perhaps you're worrying about an important speech you need to give. Maybe you're fretting about attending a big reunion party where lots of your old school or university friends might judge you. Or maybe you're lying in bed unable to sleep because you've got that big exam or test the next morning.

We are capable of feeling bad in so very many ways: angry, fearful, anxious, worried, hopeless, slightly sad or downright depressed, resentful, guilty, or ashamed. But you don't have to feel bad ever again.

Based on the principles of cognitive behavioural therapy (CBT), the FACADe technique is a powerful tool for tackling worries by distinguishing between fact and fiction, separating out what you feel from what's actually going on. Thousands of research studies involving many tens of thousands of people have proven that you can shift the way you think. Use it and you will grow your confidence.

Confidence Booster: Giving form to your thoughts

When you're stuck in the emotional dumps, sit down with a notebook and work through the five steps of the FACADe technique.

1 **Feelings**. Begin by writing down the emotions you're experiencing such as anger, despair, anxiety, envy, shame, embarrassment, and so on. Give each feeling a score from 0 to 10, depending on how strong each feeling is.

2 **Actions**. Write down how your behaviour has changed as a result of your feelings. What is it that your feelings are stopping you from doing? Or what is it that your emotions are pushing you to do? You might, for example, want to withdraw from a situation or avoid someone. Perhaps you want to shout and scream at someone. Or sit alone crying, drink yourself into oblivion, or any other number of unproductive actions.

3 **Circumstances**. Next, describe the circumstances, the situation, that has triggered your feelings. It could be something that happened in the past, is happening right now, or you're anticipating could happen in the future. It could be an event, how someone has been behaving, or even an image or memory in your mind. Whatever is making you feel upset, write it down.

4 **ANTs**. Write down the thoughts or beliefs that are popping into your head. Look out for all of those negative thoughts about yourself, those criticisms, and unhelpful comments such as 'I'm hopeless' or 'They must think that I'm a real idiot'.

5 **Defects**. Finally, look for the defects, the flaws in your thoughts. Take each of your ANTs and rate how far you actually believe each one on a scale of 0 to 10. Look for ways to challenge each ANT. Imagine what you'd say to a friend who had that thought. What's a more constructive and compassionate thought that you could replace it with instead?

The FACADe technique takes a bit of getting used to but is the most robust tool we psychologists have for obliterating those pesky negative thoughts. But make sure you *write down* your answers to the five FACADe categories – don't just ponder them. Do it and you can separate your thoughts and emotions to find your more confident self again.

If they can do it ...

Kate has been on a diet and exercise programme for the last three weeks because she wants to get in shape for the office Christmas party. Not only that, but she will hit the big 50 next year so it feels a great time to restore her confidence in herself and her body. She bought a slinky black dress a couple of weeks ago and would love to fit into it in only five weeks' time. She was making good progress but went out on Friday night with 'the girls' for a quick drink that ended up turning into quite a lot of drinks followed by a midnight burger, fries, and extra mayonnaise on the side!

She feels desperately unhappy – totally gutted that she's blown her good efforts and ruined her diet. She doesn't know if she can be bothered to make a healthy meal today or go to the gym again. What's the point? But she decides to give the FACADe technique a shot.

Here's what she writes down as she works through the five steps.

1 **Feelings**. I feel truly guilty that I let myself down (6). But I also feel ashamed (8) because I've been telling people at work for the last few weeks how much progress I've made and now they think I'm a useless pig for stuffing myself on Friday night. I'm disappointed (5) in myself too.
2 **Actions**. Well, I've been sat on the sofa all morning because I don't know if I can be bothered to go to the supermarket to trawl the aisles for healthy food. I could make a quick call and have a 14-inch pizza delivered right now that wouldn't take any effort at all. And I'm not sure if I want to go to the gym either. It's going to take another two or three gym sessions to burn off all the food I wolfed down last night.

3 **Circumstances**. It was all last night. I knew that I shouldn't have had that first drink. I knew that 'only one' would turn into two, three, and then more. And I should have known better – I always fancy a burger when I've had a few to drink!

4 **ANTs**. OK, here goes. I'm thinking:
- My friends at work think I'm a fat pig.
- I'm a useless fat pig.
- I'm never going to get into that new dress for the party.

5 **Defects**. Dr Rob's book says to look for the flaws in each ANT, so I'll take each one in turn.

Do my friends really think I'm a fat pig? No. I know Jane has tried to lose weight loads of times too so she's hardly going to laugh at me when I've been so supportive of her. And the rest of the girls really are my friends too. I'd never laugh at them if they had a rough day, so they're probably not thinking I'm a fat pig either. In any case, I know better than to try to read their minds. I'm not psychic!

I am a pig. But then again I'm not supposed to label myself. So maybe I should say that I pigged out on this occasion rather than that I'm a pig! And I shouldn't say that I'm useless either. I need to tell myself that I let myself down on this occasion – but it's the only time I've slipped up in three weeks!

I'm probably being a bit overdramatic about never getting into that dress. I still have five weeks and if I go to the gym an extra time this week, I can make up for last night's blow-out. Right, I need to get to the supermarket and buy those groceries so I can get to the gym before it closes this evening!

Yes the FACADe technique takes a bit more time to work through, but it really is very effective. Use it the next time you feel unhappy to challenge your thoughts and feelings. Use it once, then again and again. Keep using the technique, don't let your guard down too quickly. Because ANTs are stubborn little buggers, just like an ant infestation in your garden. If you don't pay attention, they can sneak back in and wreak havoc all over again. They bury themselves deep underground and it takes time to eliminate them entirely.

But if you practise the FACADe, your ANTs will stay away longer each time. With enough practice, you should be able to recognise your ANTs without writing them down. Eventually, spotting and challenging your ANTs could become a new habit, an instinct that's as natural as breathing or blinking.

You can sidestep the trap of negative thinking by cross-examining what's going on in your head. But you have to remember to use the technique when you're feeling glum or negative about yourself. I know people who write the word FACADe on sticky notes that they can post on their fridge, car dashboard, computer keyboard, and so on. How will you remember?

Taking your thoughts to task

Looking for defects in your thoughts, the fifth step of the FACADe technique, is perhaps the hardest. While you may easily name your emotions and recognise the thoughts that are running through your head, you may feel as if you don't have the right to challenge your thoughts.

To give yourself the best shot at catching the flaws in your ANTs, imagine that you're a third party – a sympathetic friend – interrogating your own beliefs. Ask yourself the following questions:

- Are you jumping to the worst possible conclusions? (For example, a friend doesn't turn up to meet you and you automatically assume that he hates you and doesn't want to see you again.) Remember that situations happen for all sorts of reasons and your automatic thought is unlikely to be the only explanation.

- Are you using words such as 'always' or 'never' to make overly sweeping statements about yourself based on a single event? (For example, failing a driving test but thinking 'I'll *never* learn to drive'.) Ask yourself whether your 'always' or 'never' statement is perhaps overdramatic based on just a handful of incidents.

- Are you predicting a terrible future rather than waiting to see what happens? (For example, 'I'm going to fail that exam' or 'My boss is bound to turn down my request – so why bother asking?') No one can predict the future, so don't do it.

- Are you labelling yourself as a failure, worthless, or useless rather than as a person who has failed? (For example, thinking 'I'm such a *failure*' rather than 'I failed on that occasion but I can try again next time'.) Remind yourself that setbacks and mistakes do not make you a failure but merely someone who needs to try a different approach next time.

- Are you trying to read someone else's mind? (For example, automatically thinking 'He's yawning so he must think I'm really boring' rather than that he might be tired.) As you can't possibly read anyone else's mind, give other people the benefit of the doubt.

- Are you using words such as 'must', 'should', 'ought', or 'have to' to make excessive demands on yourself or other people? (For example, thinking 'I must not let people down' and then lambasting yourself because you had to let someone down.) If you find yourself falling into this trap, go on to ask yourself: why? Why *must* or *should* you or anyone else *have to* do anything? Try to be more flexible with yourself.

- Are you belittling your own achievements? (For example, thinking 'That was easy – anyone could have done it' or turning a friend's positive comment on its head to think 'He's only saying that because he feels sorry for me – I'm such a loser'.) It's a tough world out there already; you don't need to rubbish your own triumphs.

Ask yourself questions and you poke holes in the unhelpful beliefs you hold. Do it often enough and you will soon feel more positive and confident about yourself and the world around you.

Looking on the bright side

Modern life is full of ambiguous meanings. From vaguely phrased emails to half-heard conversations, it's easy to jump to the wrong conclusions about other people's intentions. A friend who hasn't returned your calls might be busy rather than upset with you.

Almost any situation can be interpreted in any number of ways. Remember that your beliefs are not the same as reality. Your beliefs are just one way of thinking about a situation or set of circumstances. Beliefs are rarely 'right' or 'wrong', but they can be empowering or disempowering, constructive or destructive. So why not choose to replace a disempowering belief with a more enabling one? Believe the best about yourself and you may surprise yourself by achieving it.

The FACADe technique for challenging the nasty ANTs that scuttle into your mind is a powerful weapon in your arsenal for protecting your self-confidence. But once you've challenged and eliminated your unhelpful beliefs, you can further grow your confidence by replacing them with more positive ones.

Earlier in this chapter I suggested that six people who got rejected after a job interview could interpret it in different ways, with the result that a few felt good and most felt bad. But if six people can think about the same situation in six different ways, then one person can think about a single situation in six different ways too. The friend who hasn't returned your calls could be snowed under with work or wrestling with a personal crisis. She could have lost your number or had her mobile stolen. Maybe she is waiting until the right opportunity so that you can meet in person rather than talk on the telephone. And because you can't know for certain what is going on with her, you do yourself no favours by clinging on to the worst possible explanation.

This next Confidence Booster is about generating alternative explanations.

Confidence Booster: Pondering possibilities

Once you've listed and smashed the negative thoughts that may be dragging you down, you can replace them with more constructive thoughts that will lift your confidence.

Write out the first ANT that has been bugging you. Then write down a handful of alternative interpretations that could replace it. If you're feeling down, you may have to work hard to think of other ways of looking at the situation, but persevere with it. Hold a mini-brainstorm and write down anything that comes to mind for now. Imagine other possible explanations for the situation you're in.

- What are other possible ways of looking at the situation?

- Have you any past experiences that could suggest an alternative perspective on what's happening?

- Would you encourage a friend to think this way?

- What would you say to a friend who was feeling down about the same situation?

Think creatively and aim to come up with at least a handful of alternatives. Six is a good number, but three will do. Then choose a constructive and realistic alternative belief. Draw a big circle around your chosen new thought. Write it in big letters on a separate piece of paper; say it out loud with conviction, as if you already believe it. Developing even one realistic explanation to replace an ANT is often enough to enable you to feel better.

You may be wondering whether it's realistic to replace a negative thought with a positive one. But I'm not asking you to replace your ANT with *any* positive thought that occurs to you. I'm not suggesting you should ignore the facts and pretend that the world is a fantastic place – that would be naïve and phoney. You have to choose an alternative thought that is feasible and realistic given the evidence of the situation. But if you can find a good enough alternative explanation, you may find your confidence showing up again.

If they can do it ...

Ben, 24, works as an account manager for a computer supplies company. He had a sales meeting in which he was trying to persuade the client to buy one of his company's products. When the client turned him down, he felt really low. He blamed himself. But rather than let it crush his confidence, he used the FACADe technique to identify his ANTs. He found that his biggest and most persistent ANT was: 'I'm no good at selling.' To break free of his ANT, Ben writes down as many plausible explanations as he can think of:

- 'The client is a grumpy person and turns nearly everybody down.'
- 'I did a decent job but the client doesn't feel the timing is right to buy one of our products.'
- 'The client is having a bad day at work and I was unlucky enough to have met him today.'
- 'My company's products simply aren't right for the client; none of my colleagues could have persuaded the client to buy.'
- 'The client is a moron and couldn't grasp what I was getting at.'
- 'The client is preoccupied with problems in his personal life and isn't positively predisposed to *anyone* at the moment.'

The simple act of writing down a half-dozen explanations helps Ben to keep matters in perspective. He chooses to adopt 'I did a decent job but the client doesn't feel the timing is right to buy one of our products' as his new belief. He says it out loud a few times and finds that his mood begins to lift fairly quickly.

Nurturing a positive outlook

I'm going to toss a coin and make you an offer. Heads I give you £100 (or yen, dollars, euros, whatever you like). Tails you give me £100 (or yen, dollars, or euros). Can I tempt you to take the bet? Probably not, because the odds aren't that great.

But what if heads I give you £100 but tails you give me just £90 – would you take that bet now? Tempting, but still maybe not. We could go on, reducing the amount you'd have to lose until you were willing to take the bet.

Psychologist and Nobel prize winner Daniel Kahneman at Princeton University has found that most people would need to be offered a gain that's twice as large as the loss. So I'd put up £100 whereas you'd risk only £50.

The implication? The human mind is naturally attuned to feel loss more acutely than gain, to focus on negatives over positives, to agonise over risk rather than relish opportunity. But your outlook on life is not fixed. Science shows that you can change it.

I'm talking about optimism here. Optimists tend to look for what is good in the world, give themselves credit for their achievements, and focus on the pursuit of success. Pessimists, on the other hand, look for what is wrong in the world, attribute their achievements to dumb luck, and focus on the avoidance of failure. Which would you rather be – an optimist or pessimist?

Some people feel that having a negative outlook on life protects them. By expecting the worst, they can't be disappointed. But negativity doesn't protect you – it isolates you. If you don't believe me, try this little experiment: make yourself act in an optimistic and happy fashion with one person, and then negative and sad with another person. I'm sure you can appreciate that your attitude and outlook can affect how other people perceive you and treat you in turn. Pessimism breeds more negativity and closes doors. Optimism draws people to you and opens up opportunities you might otherwise ignore.

Over to you

Ask yourself:

- Do you have a more positive or negative outlook on life?

- What do you believe are the benefits of having your outlook on life?

- If you tend to be more negative in your outlook, what do you think are the disadvantages of the way you look at things?

Now you might think that your outlook on the world is something you are born with. But that's not right. Research has shown that whatever your current view of life, you can hone your level of optimism; you get more of what you focus on. So let's look at what's going well in your life every day.

Confidence Booster: Developing your sense of optimism

You can pass light through a prism to refract and separate out the colours of the rainbow. In a similar fashion, you can pass your experience through a more positive lens to focus on the more affirming highlights of your life.

Each evening, simply write down three things for which you feel grateful. These could be events that happened during the day, attributes you possess, relationships you have, or other good things you enjoy. Choose to interpret 'things for which you feel grateful' in whatever way you wish – I don't want to give you examples because you need to find what is noteworthy to you. You may choose to savour whatever pleasurable, enjoyable, or meaningful experiences you wish, no matter how great or small. If this was your last day on Earth, you'd probably find lots to appreciate. Write as much or as little about each one as you feel comfortable with.

I know the 'good things' technique sounds too simple, too good to be true. But there's hard science behind it. Professor Martin Seligman is one of the most respected psychologists in the world today. He and his crack team of researchers at the University of Pennsylvania compared the benefits of different techniques and found that this is the most powerful of the many they tested. Many other self-help techniques enhance confidence for a few weeks or a month. But even using this technique for just one week produces confidence-boosting effects up to six months later.

By looking out for a mere three good things a day, you train yourself to appreciate what is going well in your life. You begin to notice many more positive events, interactions, and moments. You achieve sustainable increases in your mood and confidence. Remember though to look out for three good things from *all* areas of your life – not just your work, your relation-ships, or whatever particular part of your life you want more confidence in.

Also, buy a beautiful notebook or diary in which to collect your record of positive moments. When you're feeling low, you can flick back through what you wrote in previous weeks and months, remind yourself about what's good in your life, and lift your mood and confidence.

Seeing success

If you get nervous pangs before a social event, speech, or inter-view, you may visualise terrible scenarios such as spilling a drink, blushing, or other social *faux pas*. But if you can visualise bad things happening, you can visualise good things too.

Another way to build stronger beliefs is to exploit the power of positive visualisation. If you've ever been bored and let your mind drift into a bit of a daydream – I know I have plenty of times! – you can harness the gift of visualisation.

Sports people have used visualisation for decades as a tool to enhance their performance. By picturing what they want to happen – being the first to cross the finish line, making the perfect golf swing, landing a triple Axel – they make it more likely to happen.

Hard science confirms the power of visualisation too. Stephen Kosslyn, a professor of psychology at Harvard University, used brain-scanning equipment to show that imagining a movement activates the same parts of the brain that light up during the actual movement. Specialised cells in the brain called mirror neurons are activated simply by *thinking* about an activity. From the brain's point of view, imagining an activity is very similar to executing it.

In case you're still not convinced, I'll share with you another recent piece of research. Professor Leslie Walker is a UK-based researcher looking at the effects of positive visualisation on cancer. Astonishingly, Professor Walker says that patients who can picture the treatment battling the cancer or visualise their tumours disappearing, achieve better outcomes. Think about that for a moment: visualisation can affect the progress of one of the most feared diseases in the modern world. So, how relatively easy should it be for you to use visualisation to fuel your confidence?

Run through an event in your head and you help yourself to perform at your confident best. Take that driving test, speak at a seminar, play the violin solo at a concert. Do it in your mind and prep yourself for the real thing.

Get ready to succeed

Some people have a mental block and think they can't visualise. But anyone can do it and here's a tiny example. I want you to imagine you're on your way home. You've had a long day and now you're standing in front of the door to your house. What do you see? What colour is the door? Where's the keyhole and what does it look like? Is there a letterbox, a handle or a doorknob? There you go, you can do it. Visualisation is nothing more than picturing images in your head. You *can* do it.

Confidence Booster: Using the movie screen in your head

Visualisation is like sitting back and watching the movie of the book of your life. Imagine you have been so successful in your life that someone has written a book about you. Not only that, but a movie studio has turned your book into a film. And now you're watching a segment of that film, the bit where you overcome your fears to deliver a sterling performance.

Find a quiet place for your visualisation. Get away from ringing telephones, noisy colleagues, rumbling trains, screaming kids, and give it a go.

- Think about the upcoming event or situation you want to feel more confident about. Perhaps it's asking your boss for a pay rise, making sparkling conversation at a party. Giving the toast at a wedding, serving a bunch of aces in a tennis tournament, or having a tough conversation with a loved one. Imagine the scene as if you were watching it on a movie screen.

- Begin by fleshing out how you look and what you're wearing. You'd be calm and composed, maybe smiling slightly, perhaps laughing a lot. What about your clothes? A smart suit, a sexy outfit, tennis whites and training shoes. Add the detail to how you look.

- Run the scene as you would *like* it to happen. *Imagine yourself enjoying the experience*. Envision yourself negotiating confidently with your boss, delighting your dinner date, getting rapturous applause from your audience. Remember that this is how you *want* the event or situation to go – so allow yourself to be a superstar in your mental movie.

- Play the scene back and add detail to make the mental images as vivid as possible. Add colour and depth and textures to make it breathtakingly real.

- Involve your other senses in the mental movie too. I know it's called visualisation, but now we're turning your movie into a 3D immersive experience. Hear the words you want to say and the sounds around you – the congratulations of your boss or the laughter of your fellow partygoers. Smell the leather of the interviewer's armchair. Taste the creamy cheesecake you're sharing with your loved one. Feel the weight and coldness of the trophy as you lift it over your head.

- Finally, add your emotions too. How does the scene make you *feel*? It goes without saying we're talking about positive emotions here. But do you want to feel calm and focused or excited and animated?

You need to run through your mental movie a couple of times to lock it into your mind. But that's all there is to visualisation. It's more straightforward to see your success than you might think.

Visualisation can allow all of us to enhance our readiness for that Big Event, the one you're feeling a little tense or downright anxious about. As with many of the techniques in this book, you need to practise to get better. Practising it will enable you to summon up those mental movies more easily and more vividly each time. The more effort you put into visualising a successful outcome, depicting with crystal clarity what you want to happen, the more your feelings of confidence will increase. How about you attempt it right now?

ONWARDS AND UPWARDS

■ Remember that your beliefs are merely your personal interpretation of what is happening to you – your beliefs are not the same as reality. If you have negative beliefs, you feel bad about yourself and the world. If you have positive beliefs, you feel strong and confident.

■ Your inner critic judges you more harshly than anyone else ever could. Take heart that, when you feel self-conscious, you are probably being judged by the voice in your head rather than the people around you.

■ You are not born with your beliefs. Yes, certain thoughts may pop automatically into your head. But you can make a conscious effort to challenge them and shed unhelpful notions about yourself.

■ Choose to adopt a more optimistic view of life. This isn't about putting on rose-tinted spectacles and pretending that the world is a wonderful place, but simply choosing to focus on what is good in your life rather than dwelling only on what is bad.

■ Use the potent – yet often overlooked – technique of visualisation for overcoming worries and preparing to tackle challenging situations.

■ But if you need to maintain your confidence when you're in the middle of a sticky situation, use the CAT (capability-affirming thought) technique to replace negative thoughts with more positive ones.

■ Your beliefs have built up over many years. So bear in mind that it may take repeated attempts to combat the effects of your unhelpful beliefs and replace them with more positive ones.

Behaving with confidence

"If you look confident you can pull off anything."
Jessica Alba, Hollywood actress

In this chapter you will ...

■ learn that behaving in a confident manner – even if you don't
feel confident to begin with – can actually help you to feel
more confident

■ understand ways to use your body language and tone of voice
to appear confident and instil confidence in others

■ learn simple techniques using your breathing and the release of
muscular tension to help you feel more confident

■ explore the language you use in order to weed out unassertive
words and phrases

■ learn to speak and behave more confidently by identifying and
observing role models around you.

Have you ever noticed that confident people seem to project
their personality outwards and appear larger than life? And that
people who lack self-belief seem to shrink away?

Even before most people open their mouths to speak, their body
language is broadcasting messages out about how they feel.
Their posture, hand movements, eyes and faces are constantly
transmitting bulletins about their state of mind.

You can take control of your body language and send the non-
verbal messages you want to communicate. No matter how you
feel, you can make confident body language your natural habit.
You will look and sound as if you are brimming with confidence,
as if you have confidence to spare.

But this isn't about pretending or faking confidence to pull
the wool over other people's eyes. Behaving confidently can
rewire your beliefs and feelings too. You guessed it – we're
back to that *do, think, feel* idea. If you steel yourself and use
confident body language, you can start to think confidently
and feel confident too. In case you're interested, psychologists call it the principle of retrospective rationality. Your

brain likes to believe that you're behaving in a fashion that is consistent with your beliefs. So if you start behaving as a confident person, your brain tries to explain your behaviour by forcing your mind to believe that you *are* a confident person.

To top it all, confidence is contagious. Many people – and this may include you – feel that they need confidence the most when they're performing in front of or interacting with other people. By behaving as if you are confident, you make others feel confident about you. They trust you're going to be good and are ready to notice what you're doing well rather than what you're doing badly. If beauty is in the eye of the beholder, then confidence is often in the eye of the observer. Other people can't tell what's going on in your head – whether you feel nervous or not. If you behave with confidence, they will believe you to be confident and treat you that way too.

However you look at it, behaving with confidence is a sure-fire winner.

"If you have zest and enthusiasm, you attract zest and enthusiasm. Life does give back in kind."

Norman Vincent Peale, preacher

You already know what you need to know

OK, you may not always manage to come across as confidently as you would like. Happily, you probably already know more about body language than you think.

Conjure up in your mind a couple of confident people that you know or have observed – even on television. See them in your mind's eye. Consider how they look and sound.

- How do they hold themselves?

- What are they doing with their hands?

- What expressions can you see on their faces?

- When they speak, how do they sound?

In mere moments, I'm sure you can picture very clearly the differences that confident versus less confident people convey. So let's have a look at how you can project that confident demeanour too.

Every breath you take

A lot of behaving with confidence is to do with appearing confident when you're with other people in social or work situations. But here's a technique you can use to alter your physiology well before you have to give that presentation, take your driving test, or play a piano recital.

Your mind affects your body and your body affects your mind. When we're stressed, we take fast, shallow breaths into the top part of our lungs – we pant. But by focusing on how we breathe, we can encourage our minds to feel more confident. The diaphragm is a swathe of connective tissue somewhere below the belly button that we use when we breathe in a natural way. Learn to breathe diaphragmatically and you can defuse negative emotions at will.

Confidence Booster: Diaphragmatic breathing

Practise diaphragmatic breathing at home by working through the
following steps:

- Place your right hand on your chest and your left hand on your belly
  button. Take a few short sniffs as if you're trying to identify a pleasant
  smell in the air. Or sniff as if you have a runny nose and want to stop
  it from dripping! You should feel your left hand moving – that's where
  your diaphragm is.

- Now take slow deep breaths into your belly, the bottom part of your
  lungs. Only your left hand should rise as you inhale and fall as you
  breathe out. Your right hand should remain completely still. Inhale to
  a slow count of four, and exhale to a slow count of four.

- Do this for a few minutes and you should feel very relaxed. Your
  fingers and toes may start to feel warm as your body relaxes and
  sends blood rushing to your extremities.

Practise diaphragmatic breathing and get used to using it when
you're relaxed. Then you can switch into this mode of breathing
quickly when you need it in a crunch. A lot of people reach for a
cigarette when they're stressed. But researchers Tony Schwartz
and Catherine McCarthy found that deep breathing can alleviate
stress just as effectively without inhaling a lungful of smoke!

Once you've got the hang of the basic diaphragmatic breathing
technique, you can also try this more advanced Confidence
Booster. The ABCD technique incorporates as one of its four
steps control over your breathing as a means of handling
acute feelings of tension, worry, or whatever else you may be
feeling.

Confidence Booster: Calming your emotions with ABCD

Whenever you're in the grip of negative emotions, work through these four steps. The point isn't to disregard your emotions or pretend that they don't exist; instead, this is about embracing your emotions yet moving on and allowing yourself to get on with whatever you need to do.

- **Acknowledge your feelings.** Our feelings are an integral part of what makes us human. Trying to ignore or suppress them doesn't work. So the first step is to embrace what you're feeling. Observe the bodily sensations, the thoughts and feelings you're experiencing. Spend a few moments engaging with them to understand what you're feeling. Then put a label on your emotions by saying (or whispering under your breath or even writing on a sheet of paper) whatever you're feeling. For example, 'This is a feeling of annoyance' or 'This is the feeling of fear'.

- **Breathe.** Now breathe deeply using the diaphragmatic breathing technique. Concentrate on the air filling your belly and exiting again. Anxious or unhelpful thoughts may still cross your mind, but focus on your breathing and they will have less power over you. At the same time, relax the muscles in your body. Unclench your jaw and fists; let the tension ebb away from your shoulders. Take as many breaths as you need until you feel the negative feelings beginning to subside.

- **Chuckle!** Yes, you read it right. Laugh. If you're in a public place and don't feel comfortable with laughing out loud, at least smile. Plant a wide smile on your face. Rather incredibly, experiments show that gritting your teeth and forcing yourself to smile can lighten your mood – even if you don't *want* to feel better (I'll explain more about this later on in this chapter). Remember that our behaviour can influence our moods. So even though it may go against your better judgement, smiling and laughter will still alleviate tension, help you to detach from any negative emotions, and lift your mood.

■ **Do something positive.** Now you should be ready to do whatever you need to be doing. Sure, your feelings may be telling you to run away from the situation. But by working through the first three steps, you should allow the rational part of your mind to wrest control back from the emotional part. So whether it's that party you need to go to, that date you need to go on, or that exam you need to take, tell yourself that you're going to do what you should be doing.

Sterling stances and perfect poise

I always used to wonder in the Superman films and TV shows how no one could tell that Clark Kent was the same person as the man of steel. But a big part of how the actors distinguished between the two was in how they held themselves. Superman stood upright with his chin held high and his chest puffed out. Clark Kent slumped his shoulders forward and kept his eyes focused mere inches from his own feet.

The first signal you get about someone's confidence or lack of it is in how they walk and hold themselves. Even from a distance – and long before you get close enough to make eye contact – you can see whether someone's shoulders and head are slumped in defeat or held high with conviction. Your quickest route to begin radiating confidence is to sort out your posture.

Imagine that a piece of silver string is attached to the top of your head. Now picture a giant invisible puppet master towering over you. See the puppet master pulling the string straight up. Do it right now – whether you're standing on a train platform, sitting in an aeroplane seat, soaking in a hot bath, or even sitting in a chair. Imagine that someone is pulling the silver string gently upwards. Your back is straightening and your head is lifting. The muscles in your neck are elongating. In fact, all of the muscles in your body would be lengthening to bring you up to your full height.

We all get lazy with our postures, particularly when we're tired. So try it for the next few days. Make a conscious effort to monitor your posture and imagine that puppet master gently pulling you upwards. Behave confidently and you will think confidently because your mind has no choice but to respond to what your body is doing.

Take Action: Learning from the best

You can adopt the secrets of confident body language more quickly by identifying role models who are already confident. You may know a friend who manages to be engaging and entertaining at social events. Perhaps you admire the way a particular celebrity radiates self-belief while talking on a TV chat show. Your role models could be real-life or fictional, dead or alive. When I give a speech, I bring to mind the resonant voice and manner of Captain Jean-Luc Picard (as played by classically trained actor Sir Patrick Stewart) from *Star Trek: The Next Generation*, who I think embodies confidence and gravitas.

Make sure that these are role models that you genuinely admire and respect. Don't try to copy someone you loathe! Whatever you like about your role models, scrutinise their behaviour and use it as a source of inspiration and ideas for how you can behave with confidence too. So have a think now, who has the levels of confidence that you aspire to possess? Write down the names of at least three role models and commit to observing them or digging up clips of them from TV or perhaps the internet. Then watch them carefully. What do they do with their posture, their gestures, their body language? How do they sound and precisely what words do they use? Then see if you can *adapt* the particular behaviour, words or mannerisms that you like about them to help you to present yourself as a confident person too.

Don't be a jerk

You can tell how confident people are even if they have their backs to you. Watch their hands and bodily movements. You don't see corporate hot-shots or television presenters jingling change in their pockets or scratching their heads. They don't shift their weight from one foot to the other or bite their nails. They don't tap their feet or fidget with their hands. And they don't do any of that because moving jerkily communicates restlessness. Fast, small movements look like twitches and tics, shudders and spasms. It's slow, large movements that signal confidence.

Be a smooth operator by keeping your hands still and relaxed when other people are talking. If you're not sure what to do with your hands, watch the confident people around you for ideas. But be sure to monitor yourself for danger signs like:

- fidgeting with objects such as pens, rings, or key chains
- touching your hair, face or body
- sucking your fingers or biting your nails
- and, of course, you know better than to cross your arms or even hug yourself unless you want to be seen as someone who's on the back foot.

However, *do* use your hands to illustrate points as you speak. Body language research tells us that people who use their hands when they speak are more visually arresting and psychologically engaging to listen to. But use your hands only in broad, sweeping gestures. For example, hold your palms upwards and you seem to invite and encourage others to pay attention to you.

Watch what you're doing with your feet too. Especially when sitting, people who are feeling less than fully confident often end up tapping their feet or crossing their legs. Confident men tend to sit with their feet planted flat on the floor with their legs slightly apart. Confident women tend to sit with their feet on the floor but with their knees pressed together.

Learning to move in a confident manner won't come overnight. It takes conscious effort and you may lapse occasionally into your old habits whenever you aren't thinking about your posture, hands, or feet. But stick with it and the confidence will come.

Confidence Booster: Muscling out stress

Ever had a massage and been told that your shoulders and back are knotted with tension? You aren't alone. Many people's bodies tighten and tense up when they are feeling anxious. Your shoulders bunch up towards your ears, your fists clench without you noticing, and you may even lock your jaw or grind your teeth when the pressure's on.

Standing tall is *not* the same as tightening up the muscles in your body. A good posture is long and upright, but with the muscles in your body – and particularly your shoulders and back – relaxed. You should have shoulders that are floppy enough to be able to move in a fluid fashion.

If you find yourself tensing up, work through a progressive muscle relaxation technique in the minutes before your moment in the spotlight. The idea: tense and release the muscles in your body from your head down to your toes, like running through a checklist of body parts to undo knots of tension.

- Tense the muscles in your face and jaw. Screw up your face and clench your teeth for a few seconds and then release. Let your jaw go slack and consciously relax the muscles in your cheeks, forehead and around the eyes.

- Now move on to your shoulders, back and chest, and hands. Clench your fists and tense your upper body as if you were getting ready to punch someone. Squeeze for a few seconds and release.

- Next move on to your stomach. Tighten it for all you're worth and release. Then move on to your buttocks, turning them into buns of solid steel for a few seconds.

- Focus next on your thighs. Push your feet into the ground or squeeze your knees together to tauten your thighs. And finally your feet – curl your toes into a ball and hold for a few seconds.

Practise at home until you become familiar enough with the technique to do it in other situations, whether that's on the train ride to a client or while waiting for the announcer to invite you up on stage. Once you get used to it, you'll get even more of an effect by combining it simultaneously with diaphragmatic breathing too.

Fake it until you make it

Here's a question for you: do you smile because you're happy or does smiling cause you to become happy?

If you think that people smile because they're happy, you'd be right. But research tells us that people who smile even when they don't feel happy initially actually become happier too. So if you guessed that, you'd also be right. Isn't that great? A question where we can all be right!

Psychologists back in the 1970s ran experiments in which they asked people to frown or smile for a few minutes even if they didn't feel happy or sad. Lo and behold. The people who frowned felt sadder. The people who smiled became happier. The simple act of smiling kick-starts your nervous system and opens the floodgates for a bunch of feel-good hormones.

So if you want to banish a foul mood and boost your confidence, force yourself to smile. For an instant pick-me-up, positively grin and beam at yourself for a few minutes. Even if it doesn't feel natural at first, do it until your face starts to ache. Maybe even laugh out loud a couple of times. I know people who keep cuttings of favourite cartoons in their desk drawers or links to humorous sites online to get them smiling. Yes, you will feel odd at first – and I'd recommend doing this somewhere away from prying eyes if you don't want people shaking their heads in puzzlement at you.

Think back to the *do, think, feel* loop. If you *do* smiling, you *think* about the concept of happiness and *feel* happier and more confident. I've heard it said: it's *easy* to laugh when things are going well, but it's *important* to laugh when things are going wrong. So put your faith in those scientists from the 1970s and your faith will be rewarded.

Looking how you'd like to feel

Whether you're going out on a date or trying to get noticed at work, you can further help yourself to feel more confident by thinking about your appearance and how you dress. In an ideal world, we would be able to say that it's what's on the inside that counts. In reality though, we know that we judge people by appearances. I do a lot of one-to-one coaching on issues including job hunting and career change, confidence-building and setting up a new business. Imagine if you came to me for a consultation and I turned up in my baggy, slightly ripped jogging bottoms and the fleece I wear for walking the dog – you wouldn't be too impressed, would you?

Our appearance is important because how we look determines how people treat us. If people are sneering at you for your untidy or outdated appearance, that's hardly going to bolster your confidence, is it?

Take Action: Dressing for success

You may already have a favourite outfit that makes you feel confident. But why limit yourself to just one or two best outfits? So turn to a few of your closest friends for advice. Pick the friends you consult based on two criteria. First, you must feel that they have supported and encouraged you in the past and never dismissed you or your intentions. Secondly, you must admire them for their sense of style *in the situations in which you want to feel more confident*. For example, a friend who can comment on appropriate attire for an interview or new job may not be the right person to help you with clothes for parties and dating.

Then ask them for advice on:

- Your wardrobe. Perhaps invite your friends to your home one weekend to chuck out the items you really should never wear. Then go out together to find some new outfits that you feel both comfortable *and* confident in – they don't have to be expensive or overly fussy to look good and make you feel good about yourself.

- Your hairstyle – is it time for a tidy-up or perhaps a fresh look?

- Your make up (if appropriate). It may have been fashionable just a few years ago, but does it need brightening up or toning down?

- Your accessories. For example, do you have glasses that make you look older than you are? Are you carrying an old briefcase or handbag that makes you look unfashionable rather than professional?

Don't take their comments personally – remember that you've enlisted them to help you! Then take the steps you need in order to feel the confidence you deserve.

The windows to the soul

Eye contact matters. Whether you're negotiating a deal with a client, asking someone out on a date, or giving a speech to a roomful of wedding guests, you need to look others in the eye. Confident people make bold eye contact. Avoid people's gaze and you look either shifty or nervous or both.

But there's a fine line between eye contact and staring. The golden rule is to look other people in the eye when *they* are speaking. However, you can look away when *you* are speaking. If you watch other people, you'll notice that their eyes flick away from yours when they have to think about what they're saying or when they're describing an image or idea that they have in their heads.

Those psychologists from the 1970s looked at eye contact too. And they found that you should typically look at someone for at least 80 to 90 per cent of the time when you're listening. But when it's your turn to speak, drop your amount of gaze to around 50 per cent. Look for too long when you're speaking and you risk coming across as slightly deranged. But look too little and you come across as shy.

Of course, I don't expect you to count the seconds you look at other people. Simply be aware of what you're doing with your eyes to enable you to create a more confident demeanour.

Sounding confident: when less is more

The way people speak often conveys more about their state of mind than the words they choose. People who speak too quietly get labelled 'quiet as a mouse'. Speak in a high-pitched voice and you are 'squeaky like a mouse'. You don't want that to be you, do you?

> "Powerful people speak slowly and subservient people quickly – because if they don't speak fast nobody will listen to them."
>
> Sir Michael Caine, actor

Let's help you convey the confidence of a lion rather than a mouse. When it comes to projecting an aura of confidence with your voice, the trick is simple to remember: speak slow, low, and loud.

Think about confident people that you know. Play back in your head what it's like to be in their presence. How do they sound? Chances are, they are loud and clear. They don't mumble or mutter or speak so quietly that you strain to make out the words. They don't screech in a pitchy voice that can only be heard by dogs and cats. Neither do their words tumble over themselves so quickly that one word crashes into the next.

So, speak slow, low, and loud. Let's look at what that means in practice.

- Let's start with the *slow* bit. Manage your pace. Make a conscious effort to slow down what you say. You can not only speak each sentence more slowly but also try to take a slightly longer pause between the end of one sentence and the beginning of the next. Allow a pause of several heartbeats, take a breath, choose your words with care, then speak.

- Think about the *pitch* of your voice too. Confident people don't squeal or screech or giggle. They speak in low, deep tones. Of course your voice has a natural range and I only suggest that you speak in the lower part of that register rather than force your voice artificially lower than it should go.

- Finally, think about your *volume*. Confident people speak loudly. And you probably need to as well. If you don't believe me, ask the opinion of your closest friends. Beg them to tell you the truth. Could you do with speaking more loudly at times?

It sounds simple enough. But don't expect to become a more confident speaker immediately. It may feel unnatural at first. You may grimace at the sound of your own voice and feel that you sound strange or too loud. But I'm willing to wager that you actually sound better to everyone else. So give it time. You're trying to overcome the habits of a lifetime. Remind yourself *slow, low and loud* every time you go into a meeting, make a telephone call, or talk to someone at a party, and you will soon find yourself conveying a powerful sense of confidence.

To help you articulate your words and speak more loudly and clearly, use this fun technique to warm up your lips, throat, and tongue for whatever your main event might be. A famous theatre director taught me it. It's especially handy if you mumble or stutter when the pressure's on.

Find a place where you won't be overheard and practise sounding out the following syllables in a loud, clear fashion.

- **'Puh buh'** – the 'p' and 'b' sounds warm up the front of your mouth and lips.

- **'Kuh guh'** – these two hard consonant sounds warm up the back of the throat and tongue.

- **'Tuh duh'** – these two sounds warm up the middle bit of your mouth including the tip of your tongue.

Exaggerate the movement of your lips and face so you can feel the muscles working. Ideally, do it in front of a mirror so you can see your lips and face moving. Start softly on one of the pair of syllables and repeat it at least a dozen times (e.g. 'puh buh, puh buh, puh buh ...' and so on), getting slightly louder each time until you are almost spitting the sounds out.

Remember to breathe diaphragmatically as well. Taking deep breaths into your belly will help you to speak with more volume and for longer without having to draw breath.

What are your words worth?

Early in my career, I ran a workshop with a colleague. I opened the workshop and spoke for about half an hour. I thought it went well. But my colleague told me that in the first 10 minutes alone, I had said 'you know' over 40 times. And then she got bored and stopped counting.

I was mortified and really annoyed with myself. But it was a great lesson. Because many people use verbal fillers such as 'sort of', 'like', 'I mean', or 'you know'. Words and phrases that add nothing to a conversation. That exist only to pad out the words that matter.

Look out for your own verbal fillers. 'Er' and 'um' are the two most common ones, but also beware of phrases such as:

- 'I'm *only* the office manager'
- 'It's *just* a hobby of mine'
- 'I *hope* that we can meet up again'.

Look out for 'just', 'only' and 'I hope' – words that make you appear weak. So get rid of them. And think about everything you say. Throw out 'I'll try' and say instead 'I will'. Rather than saying 'I don't think that I like ...', why not say 'I know that I ...'? Don't say 'I'm afraid I won't be able to come to the meeting' – why be 'afraid' of anything? Just say 'I can't come to the meeting'.

You can use more positive language. After I learnt that I used 'you know' all the time, I felt more self-conscious for a while. Every time I said 'you know', my inner critic reared up and made me feel stupid. But it got better. By taking a deliberate pause before speaking and making a conscious effort to choose my words with more care, I drove the dreaded phrase from my vocabulary.

Ask a friend to lend a hand in eliminating unassertive words and phrases from your language. Tell your confidant to observe you the next time you speak – perhaps in a meeting at work or a social situation with friends. Afterwards, ask for feedback on any words and phrases that may signal a lack of confidence. Learn what you do wrong and you can start getting it right.

Donald, 55, is a regional director for a high street bank. He is responsible for over 400 bank branches and nearly 6,000 staff. However, he came to me for coaching because he felt that his career had stalled. He had noticed that other regional directors were being promoted ahead of him despite them delivering less in terms of business results. He had so far tried to let his achievements speak for themselves, but it was clear that they were not speaking strongly enough. After some discussion, we agreed that he needed to do more to raise his profile and build stronger relationships with the most senior people within the bank who could promote him.

He started observing his colleagues to identify how people behaved to promote themselves. He became aware of key behaviours that he could engage in to help his achievements get noticed.

One key behaviour was simply to speak up more in meetings. He noticed that the colleagues who spoke up most in team meetings seemed to gain favour with the senior managers. Almost regardless of the value of their contributions, the mere act of speaking up was held in high regard by the people who mattered. So he set a goal to speak up more during meetings. As someone who did not always have the confidence to speak spontaneously, he scrutinised how other people spoke. He started taking time before meetings to prepare possible comments and questions that he could raise seemingly off-the-cuff.

He also noticed that many of his peers were more active in visiting the bank's head office in London. He tended to travel to the head office only when it was strictly necessary. Yet he discovered that many of his counterparts were travelling even longer distances than he had to, under the pretext of updating their bosses on what they were doing, but perhaps more importantly, building interpersonal relationships.

By making a handful of simple changes to his behaviour, Donald feels confident that he is a strong contender for promotion when it next becomes available.

Translating your understanding into actions

You get the idea about behaving with confidence. But how about the practice?

Changing your behaviour is both incredibly simple and surprisingly tough. It's simple in that it's easy to understand. Standing up straighter or speaking more loudly is not difficult in the same way that performing complex calculations in your head is difficult. But it's tough in the same way that changing any habit is.

Think about giving up smoking. The theory is simple enough. You throw the cigarettes in the bin and never pick 'em up again. But so many people struggle to give up cigarettes because they have become used to picking up a cigarette first thing in the morning, or having one with a coffee or a beer with friends.

And the same goes for the ingrained habits that may in the past have led you to speak or behave in a less-than-confident manner. The concepts behind what you need to do from now on are easy to grasp. But it takes constant vigilance on your part to make these new habits stick. If you want to get better at behaving with confidence, you need to practise it. Do it again and again. Then again and again some more.

Over to you

Some people make the mistake of trying to do too many things at once when working on confident body language. Better to work on a few behaviours and master them completely before moving on to other ones. So what *three* behaviours are you going to work on to begin with?

- ....

- ....

- ....

Listing the handful of changes you want to make is a great start. Perhaps you want to feel more confident when socialising or being more assertive with people you love. Maybe you want to behave with confidence when networking or selling to clients or speaking in public or anything else. Whatever you want, read on in the next chapter to discover how to set yourself a SPOT goal that will allow you to conquer that skill.

ONWARDS AND UPWARDS

- Learning to behave with confidence is often half of the battle when it comes to feeling more confident. Behave in a confident manner and – even if you don't feel confident at first – you can help to rewire how you think and feel about yourself.

- Your posture sends secret messages to other people about how you feel. Imagine that you have a piece of silver string attached to the top of your head that is constantly pulling you to stand up straight, tall, and proud.

- Look around you to identify confident people. Make a mental note of what they seem to say or do – what can you learn from them and incorporate into your own repertoire of behaviour?

- Practise the diaphragmatic breathing and muscular relaxation techniques until you are able to wind down your body at will.

- Don't expect results overnight. Remember that it takes practice and a bit of patience to unlearn bad habits and adopt new ones.

04

Setting confident goals

"If one advances confidently in the direction of his dreams, and endeavours to live the life which he has imagined, he will meet with a success unexpected in common hours."

Henry David Thoreau, author

In this chapter you will ...

■ identify the personal strengths that help you to perform at your best

■ create a picture of a confident future to motivate you into action

■ uncover the personal values that will allow you to live a contented and confident life

■ set effective goals that you will actually want to achieve

■ take practical steps to creating the more confident you.

The Spice Girls are the biggest-selling all-female pop group in history. Their debut single 'Wannabe' sold millions worldwide despite some ropey lyrics. I'm sure you know the song – the one that tells you 'what I want, what I really really want'. And then you find out that what they 'really really really' want is a 'zigazig ha'.

Excuse me? I'm not even sure if 'zigazig ha' is a verb or a noun, an action or a thing. But whatever it is, the Spice Girls really, really want it. So what do *you* really, really want?

There's a saying that you can do *anything*, but you can't do *everything*. If you don't set goals, you end up aimless, adrift, perpetually scattering your energy in 20 directions and going nowhere. With goals, you can set a clear direction, make plans, and take action.

If you're like most people, you've made New Year's resolutions in the past. Maybe to get in better shape, get a new job, be more sociable, quit a bad habit, save more money – you know the kind of thing. But, still assuming you're like most people, you've failed to keep them too. We're all busy and other stuff ends up getting in the way; so we lapse back into old, bad habits.

The good news is that a solid foundation of research and practice shows how to set effective goals that you will be looking forward to achieving. And so I'm going to share these tips with you to help you get what you really, really want.

Peering into the crystal ball

Wouldn't it be great to be able to see the future? To know the next set of lottery numbers, what's going to happen to house prices, and how your job, relationship, health, children, and everything else will turn out. Of course no one can. But you can do the next best thing: you can *create* your own future.

Confident people do not merely wait for the future to unfold – they make the future happen. If they want the top job and the corner office, they figure out what they must achieve to get it. If they want to settle down and start a family, they create the opportunities to meet a prospective partner. And that's what you're going to do too. You are going to take control of your life by creating a vision of the life you want.

'Vision?' I hear you ask. A vision is simply a picture of where you would like your life to go. If life is a journey, what's *your* destination? When you know you are heading for a worthwhile future, you start to see the predicaments and obstacles you encounter as mere inconveniences on the way to achieving your future. You feel in control and confident because you know that your actions are moving you towards your vision.

Most confident people have a vision of where they want to go – not a rigid plan but at least a broad direction. They may not call them visions, but that doesn't mean that they don't have them. They may think of them as long-term goals, plans, or ambitions. Or their sense of purpose and meaning in life. But the point is that they have them.

Get ready to succeed

Start to collect a mental dossier of people you admire – perhaps friends, colleagues, people in the public eye, or even people from history or fiction that you've read about. Consider what it is about each of them you admire. Ask yourself: what does that tell you about what you want in your own life?

A vision inspires you to make plans and take action. Having a vision is like booking a holiday. When it comes to choosing a holiday destination, you have so many choices. You could ski in Aspen, walk in the Lake District, shop in New York, sightsee in Beijing, trek in India, sun-worship in the Bahamas. But you can't plan or get excited about it until you make a decision and know where you're going. Only when you can see yourself sipping a cocktail on the beach or feeling the crunch of fresh snow under your boots can you get *really* fired up. Only then can you make plans about what to pack, how to get there, what jabs you might need, what you want to do, where you want to visit. And in the meantime if you have a bad day, you only need bring to mind your impending holiday to make yourself feel warm and cheery inside.

And that's what your vision can do for you. Your vision is there to:

■ excite you and inspire you to make plans

■ remind you of the brilliant future that could be yours

■ keep you motivated and working towards it until you achieve it.

The human being is the only animal that can think about the future, so you may as well use that talent. Whether your long-term aspirations are to be confident and popular in your social life or a successful business person, a winning sports player or a great parent, you need a vision to get you there.

Over to you

Vision is big stuff, but you can start off smaller. I call this one the Tombstone Test.

- In 10 words or less, write down: what motto would you like inscribed on your tombstone?

- What does your chosen phrase say about what you would like to achieve and be remembered for in your life?

"As long as you are going to think anyway – you might as well think big!"

Donald Trump, entrepreneur

Celebrating your strengths

Creating a vision isn't quite the same as daydreaming about a fantasy life. Sure, I'd like to be a kick-ass international superspy like James Bond or Jason Bourne but that's not very likely to happen. I've been on a shooting range and I know I'm fairly below average with a gun. I'd be no good at hand-to-hand combat and I know I don't work well under pressure!

The kinds of visions that help us to succeed in life *have to be grounded in reality*; they have to acknowledge our strengths, our natural talents, what we're good at. We all have unique strengths and we can all perform more confidently when we can play to those strengths.

Think about the strengths that make up a football team. Imagine a football team with a great centre forward and a superb goalkeeper. What would happen if the team manager put the goalkeeper into the centre forward position and the centre forward into goal? Can you imagine how the two players would perform? Badly, almost certainly. Do you suppose that the two players would feel confident in their new roles? No, probably not.

People are more confident *and* successful when they focus on their strengths rather than dwell on their weaknesses. If you play to your strengths in creating a vision of the life you'd like to lead, you give yourself the best shot at achieving it.

I'm sure you know from personal experience that investing your energies in an activity you are good at is much more fun than working on one of your hated weaknesses. Off the top of your head, what are the tasks you hate doing? And what stuff do you get a kick out of?

Many people downplay their talents. But just because a talent comes naturally to you does not mean that it comes easily to others. Perhaps you pick up foreign languages quickly. Maybe you impress friends and family with your cooking. Or you are the technology whiz who is always sorting out everyone else's computers, or the sympathetic ear whenever people have problems. Whatever your talents, you probably feel knowledgeable, strong, and in control when you deploy them.

No one can be good at everything. And confident people know that they need to give themselves credit for their strengths rather than beat themselves up for their weaknesses. You don't think David Beckham gives himself a hard time for not being a good goalie, do you? If your life is a game of football, let's identify your strengths and figure out what position would best suit you.

"The same man cannot be well skilled in everything; each has his own special excellence."

Euripides, Greek dramatist

Over to you

To help you identify your strengths, here are the beginnings of two statements:

■ I am good at ....

■ I enjoy ....

Copy them out and complete them *at least* 10 times each – yes, 10. Most people are too modest about their strengths so you may need to overcome your overly humble nature. Think about all of the different areas of your life. Your strengths may lie in how you handle people, numbers, facts, animals, plans, food, technology, ideas, fashion, yourself, or anything else you can think of. Capture every strength that comes to mind – no matter how mundane or trivial you think it may be. Once you've written down all of your statements, have a look back at them. What do you see?

Give it a shot right now. Take just five minutes to complete the sentence stems on a fresh sheet of paper. Soon you'll find new strengths tumbling out of your head. But if you get stuck for inspiration, why not get your family and friends to help? Meet for a coffee, pick up the telephone, or drop them an email to explain that you've taken on a personal development project. Perhaps pose a question on Facebook and see what your friends say. Ask them: 'What do you think I'm good at?'

I'm willing to bet that your friends and family are more positive about what you can do than you are about yourself. So it won't be long before you have plenty of ideas about your strengths.

When you have more time, try this next, more in-depth strengths exercise too. The aim of the exercise is to reminisce about the good times you had in your life. Doing so may help you to identify strengths that you may have used at different stages in your life.

Do take your time with it though. It's not to be done in one sitting. A good way to kick it off is by flicking through old photo albums to remind yourself of the good times you've had over the years, the people you were with, the fun you had. Perhaps have a glass of wine as you settle on your sofa with a notebook and pen. Or sit down in front of your computer with a steaming mug and a croissant. Revisiting past achievements should be fun!

Take Action: Telling the story of your strengths

Being able to use your strengths regularly will help you to be successful as well as satisfied. However, we can sometimes get side-tracked into different avenues that take us away from our strengths. People often find that they felt most fulfilled at some earlier stage in their lives. So this story-telling exercise enables you to track down strengths you may have forgotten you have.

Take yourself back in time to the first year of your childhood that you can remember with any clarity. Some people may only be able to recall the details from their late teenage years while others may be able to remember back to when they were as young as 7 or 8 years of age. Write down the year of your earliest memories at the top of a fresh page.

1 **Outline what happened to you that year.** Jot down a few points to remind yourself where you lived, who you spent time with, and what you spent your time doing. Old photos can be really helpful in jogging your memory.

2 **List your personal highlights for that year.** Write down every high point you experienced or success you achieved. Keep your definition of success as broad as possible to include everything you accomplished, were responsible for, overcame, were proud of, or enjoyed – no matter how large or small. You only need to write a couple of words or a sentence on each at this stage. But aim for at least two or three triumphs for the year.

3 **Then move on to the next year.** Go back to step 1 and 2 for every year of your life until you catch up with the present day.

4 **Pull out your favourite moments.** For each of your most cherished highlights or the successes that you took most pleasure from, write a paragraph describing what you did. Write in the first person ('I did …') as if you are telling a friend the story of what you did. Focus mainly on the actions and decisions you took – what you did, said, and made happen – that turned the situation into a memorable moment.

5 **Look at the *verbs* in your stories.** Look at the decisions you made and the actions you took. What talents did you exercise to achieve each success? Your strengths could be anything. You may feel strong when listening to other people, making others feel valued, analysing problems, working with animals, understanding technology, making plans, or showing integrity. Perhaps you feel strong when creating with your hands, inspiring others, negotiating deals, demonstrating empathy, challenging the status quo, serving others, and so on.

This exercise may take a bit of time, but it's worth doing. Remember to take your time to do it over several days or a couple of weekends rather than trying to do it in one session. It can be enjoyable to reminisce about past achievements and fun times. Plus, it will boost your confidence to remind yourself of past accomplishments and the skills you have.

Remember that much of the value of this book is in the doing, not the reading. Sure, you understand the concept of identifying your strengths, but understanding is not execution. Only when you know your strengths can you find roles – both in work and outside of it – that will help you to feel most confident.

If you're interested in finding out more about your personal strengths, I've written an entire book on the subject too. *Personality: How To Unleash Your Hidden Strengths* (also by Prentice Hall Life) contains seven quizzes to help you identify your unique pattern of strengths and gives you plenty more advice on how to build a confident and successful future.

Crafting a confident future

Now it's time to pull together your vision. Your vision should be an inspirational picture of your future – how you'd *like* your life to turn out rather than how it is *likely* to turn out. Because your vision should include everything you want to achieve in life, it should feel at least a little scary, but hopefully also awe-inspiring. Get it right and your vision should put a big smile on your face every time you think about it.

Ready to give it a try?

Take Action: Creating your vision

Your future can be better than your past or present. Dream big. If your life could go as well as it possibly could, what would it look like?

Come on, this is your chance. Make sure you're in a positive and upbeat mood before you start this exercise. Perhaps engage in a favourite activity beforehand so you feel calm and optimistic.

Then find a time and place where you can enjoy a half-hour or so of uninterrupted thought. Envisage a special birthday party thrown in your honour, say five or ten years in the future. See in your mind's eye a momentous occasion with all of the key people in your life there to celebrate with you. This is a special gathering because it marks a decade since you decided to change your life. You have worked hard, overcome hurdles, and achieved the goals you set yourself. Now hear the joy and laughter in the air. See the glasses raised to toast the person that you are, the life that you have lived, and the successes you have achieved. You have asked a handful of the most important people in your life to give speeches in your honour. What would they say about you?

Formulate your own vision by working through the following steps:

1 Let your imagination go a little wild. Avoid merely extrapolating your current life into the future. Your vision should capture a sense of what is *possible*, not what is *probable*. Imagine that the next ten years have gone well. How would that future look and feel?

2 Think about the handful of key people you would like to be giving speeches about you. Choose people who would be able to speak about the different areas of your fantastic life.

3 Write down in detail what you would like each of them to say about you. Think about the eight spheres of a confident life from Chapter 1: your physical health, intimate relationships, family and social life, career, money, purpose in life, and fun. Remember also your strengths from the exercise earlier on in this chapter. Each speech should aim to capture not only your achievements but also the strengths you used to get where you are.

4 Consider your response to all of the speeches. As the guest of honour, you can't get away without sharing your thoughts about your journey over the last decade. What would you say? What are the highlights you want to comment on? How did you use your strengths to get where you are? And how does it *feel* to be where you are now?

If they can do it ...

Alex, 28, has been working as an assistant manager for a high street retailer for four years. He has a comfortable life, renting a room from a married couple, and he has a solid group of friends. However, he feels both bored and frustrated with his work, with being single, with not having enough money to get his own place. And he realises that if he doesn't do something, he could easily become a 38-year-old assistant manager living the same life, renting a room, feeling the same way.

But no longer. He decides to take control. He writes out how he would like his future to turn out.

It's my 40th birthday party and my friends, family and girlfriend are gathered with me to celebrate. And it's a double celebration as the boss of the technology consultancy that I work for last week asked me to become a partner in the firm.

My dad is the first to stand and speak: 'Happy birthday son. I am so proud of you. When you were in your late 20s, I felt that you were drifting and that you could have easily coasted into your 30s and 40s and the rest of your life without achieving anything of note.'

'Of course I'm proud of your career achievements. Going back to college to take that software engineering course was the beginning of turning your life around. But what I'm most proud of is that you've made such an effort with your family. You seem to have spent your 20s pulling away from the rest of us, but now you're a fantastic uncle to your nephews and nieces. And you still come home to visit your dear old parents! Happy birthday again and I hope that it won't be long before you are tying the knot with your better half too.'

Next to toast my success is my close friend Peter: 'Happy birthday you old dog. I really didn't think you'd amount to anything. I thought you were going to be the same old Alex forever, always needing to borrow a few pounds until the end of the month, which I knew I'd never get back. But here we are celebrating in this magnificent house. Your kitchen is bigger than my entire flat!'

'But the combination of your studying and hard work has paid off and you deserve everything that you've got now. Well done and enjoy your day!'

Finally, my boss and friend (I'm going to call him William) finishes off the toasts: 'I hired you because you struck me as a young man who was determined to succeed. Yes, you had your critics who said that you hardly had any experience. But you impressed us with the ferocious determination in your eyes. You told me that if I hired you, you'd work whatever hours it took to get the job done. And you've been as good as your word. So I am proud and very pleased to be able to celebrate both your birthday and the fact that you will as of January be a full partner in the firm. Congratulations!'

Even if you don't have a half-hour right now to write out your vision, you can certainly spend a few minutes daydreaming. Allow yourself to wonder about your ideal future life. Go on, do it now. Close your eyes or gaze out of the window and let your mind's eye fast forward into the future:

- What are you doing?

- Who are you with?

- What's going on at work and outside of it?

Let your imagination off its leash. Just make sure you're not operating heavy machinery while you're doing it!

What's the *worst* thing that could happen if you pursue your vision? Well, you may not achieve it; you may end up where you are now. But what's the *best* thing that could happen if you pursue your vision? Imagine if you achieved it *all* ...

Picture perfect

Here's an alternative idea for you. Your vision is a picture of the future, so why not draw it if you like? You may have heard that most people favour either the left- or right-side of their brain. Left-brainers think in a logical, linear fashion and typically prefer writing to drawing. Right-brainers are more creative and more switched on by images than words.

I'm a left-brainer. I feel strong writing my thoughts down and uncomfortable when drawing or being the slightest bit creative. But I know right-brainers who love images and feel stifled by words. If you want to create your vision in a form other than words, do it. Cut out pictures from magazines to fill a scrap book or create a collage. Draw a representation of your vision or turn it into a comic strip. Create a papier mâché sculpture of it or shoot a video diary of yourself. Do what works for you. Just make sure you do it.

Living an authentic life

Remember this is your vision, your life. Your vision should capture your authentic aims and ambitions and not those of your friends or colleagues, parents or siblings, neighbours or anyone else. Many people find themselves being influenced by what they think they *should* or *ought to* do. But someone else's bliss could be your personal drudgery.

Don't settle for what you have just because everyone else seems to be doing it. Don't get a mortgage and put down roots because you're expected to. So what if everyone else is chasing a bigger salary and flashy job title if that's not what you want? Enough! You have to say the hell with everyone else's expectations and decide to live your life how you want. Go for what *you* want rather than what seems socially acceptable. True confidence comes from pursuing your own dreams and not those of the people around you.

"I don't know the key to success, but the key to failure is to try to please everyone."

Bill Cosby, comedian

Vision or daydream?

A vision is a motivating picture of what you hope to *achieve* because achieving distinguishes a vision from a mere daydream. A daydream is just an idle thought with no actions, no results, while a vision inspires you to take action.

The difference between a vision and a daydream

Vision	Daydream
Depends on your efforts	Depends on luck (e.g. 'I wish I could win the lottery' or 'I wish a talent scout would discover me')
Puts you in control	Allows others to take control
Encourages you to take responsibility for making things right	Allows you to blame other people or circumstances for things being wrong
Creates the right circumstances	Waits for circumstances to be right
Inspires you to create a plan of action	Enters your thoughts occasionally but never for long
Is achieved through a little effort every day	Is realised in an unlikely flash or instant
Requires action today	Puts off action for another day

The choice is yours. If you only *wish* you could change, shrug your shoulders and do nothing, then the only person you let down is yourself. Take charge. Put this book down right now and *do* something. Even if it's only to reach for a pen to capture your ideas on paper, take action!

Leading a life worth living

"This above all: to thine own self be true."

William Shakespeare, playwright

What do you value? What's important to you? If you could only be or have one thing, what would it be? It's a big question – real 'meaning of life' stuff. In fact, it *is* about the meaning of life: what's the meaning of *your* life?

Values are a set of standards or guidelines, a code of conduct, for how people live their lives. People who are spiritual might call it their morals or mores. Others might call it their attitude to or philosophy of life. But what you call it is less important than what it allows you to do. Your values are what matters to you, what you care about and hold dear. People who live according to their values are fulfilled, confident and contented. People who have to compromise on their values feel frustrated if not downright depressed.

Now you may think that sounds a bit grand. That you don't live your life by any rules or principles. If you're like most people, you probably don't spend a lot of time thinking about your values. But that doesn't mean you don't have them.

Say you work for a boss who treats people like dirt because the only thing that matters to him is making money. If that rubs you the wrong way, perhaps your values are more to do with people – or at least not so much about making money at all costs. Or a friend of yours is always forgetting to return your calls. If that annoys you to your core, then you probably have a value that is something to do with keeping your promises or being loyal to friends. When you approve or disapprove of the actions and circumstances of the people around you, that's often a good indicator as to what your values may be.

Confident, successful people have a vision *and* know their values – and so should you. Your vision mostly depicts what you would like to achieve. But your values define what you are and aren't willing to do, how you will and won't behave, to achieve it.

You may not currently be living your life according to your values. Life isn't always easy and people have to make compromises to get themselves through the day. But once you've identified your values and begun to live by them, you will experience a new sense of freedom. You can let go of stuff that isn't important to you and instead focus only on what matters.

Over to you

Your values may be more important to you than you realise. Identify a time when your values were put to the test. Consider the following:

■ What was the situation?

■ What did you do or how did you feel?

■ What did you learn about yourself and your values?

Take Action: Uncovering your values

The following is a list of possible values. Some are tangible values, including wealth and possessions. A few describe situations or circumstances such as security and geographical location. Others are personal characteristics such as integrity and kindness. Which ones stand out as being of the greatest importance to you? Start by circling however many you like or copying them out onto a fresh sheet of paper.

Friends	Influence	Accomplishment	Personal growth
Challenge	Contribution to society	Creativity	Respect
Predictability	Family	Integrity	Excitement
Excellence	Status	Kindness	Autonomy
Authority	Solitude	Helping others	Fun
Loving partner	Humour	Stability	Loyalty
Being needed	Personal possessions	Peace	Being attractive
Learning	Health	Responsibility	Security
Freedom	Adventure	Spiritual growth	Success
Control	Making a difference	Routine	Sporting ability
Your faith	Honesty	Equity ownership	Location
Recognition	The environment	Being wanted	Children
Independence	Affiliation	Love	Community
Power	Travel	Art/aesthetics	Wealth

No list of values could ever be comprehensive. Add whatever other words or phrases you feel could better capture what you value. Think about people you work or socialise with as well as people you've read or heard about. What do you like about how they live their lives? What do they do that you wish you could do too?

You may feel that many of these values play a part in your life. To be useful though, you need to identify your *core* values. Your values should help you to weigh up alternatives and make better choices. If a choice takes you away from or against one of your values, you know immediately to find another route to take. But if you have too many values, you can't make effective decisions. Practically speaking, a list of more than 10 or so values is little better than having none at all. Ten values should be your maximum but fewer are even better.

Think about what each value means to you. Is it an integral part of your life or merely a nice-to-have? How would you feel if it were taken away from you?

Next, turn each of your core values into a guideline that you can follow, live your life by, and make decisions with. How do you see that value steering your behaviour? For example, three different people who each include 'family' in their set of values could create different rules as follows:

- ◼ 'I put my family first in *everything* I do. Even if my career prospects suffer as a result, but so long as I earn enough money to put a roof over their heads and food on the table, my family knows that they always come first.'

- ◼ 'I spend every Saturday with my family. That doesn't mean that I need to give up what I love (like going to home rugby matches). But if I'm to do the things I love, I have to persuade – not force – my family to be a part of my activities too.'

- ◼ 'I put my family at the heart of everything I do, but I'm not going to be unrealistic about it. I aim to spend at least three evenings a week getting home from work early enough to eat with them, read to the children, and put them to bed. If I can't do that occasionally, I'm not going to punish myself over it.'

Your final step is to rank your values statements. You could write your shortlist of values on sticky notes and shuffle the list around until you have your most deeply cherished value at the top. Or simply rewrite your list, numbering them in order of priority.

Avoid, if you can, having tied rankings in your list of values. Life often involves trade-offs. We only have 24 hours in the day and you can't be in two places at once. If you want to be rich, you may have to say no to social and personal relationships more times than you would like. If you crave excitement and adventure in your life, you may not be able to make as much money as your peers. If you want to be remembered above all for your kindness, you may have to sacrifice honesty and go along with the occasional white lie.

I'm not suggesting that you concoct a list of prescriptive rules and live your life in a regimented or inflexible way. Your values are a set of guidelines – not regulations – and it's up to you to interpret them in different situations. But by identifying your deep-seated values, you can weigh up options and opportunities to see which ones sit best with your principles. You can allocate time and energy to tasks and situations that matter to you and remove yourself from ones that don't. People in history have died for their values; you can at least learn to make better choices and occasionally say no to people because of yours.

If they can do it ...

Nina, 41, works as a recruitment consultant. She is financially successful but recently has found herself getting irritable with colleagues and clients. Realising that her passions lie elsewhere, she wrote a vision and decided that she would love to run a restaurant. She recognises that this is a long-term goal that may take her a number of years, but in the meantime she uncovers her values to sustain her until she achieves her vision.

After selecting an initial list of over a dozen values, she pares them down to a final five. And here are the statements she writes to guide how she aims to live.

- **Excitement**. 'I want a fresh challenge every day. I'd rather earn less but be entertained and surprised by what happens every day at work than be rich but bored.'

- **Affiliation**. 'Having people around me that I like and trust is critical in all areas of my life. When I set up to do whatever I end up doing, I will do it in partnership with other people. I'd rather be part of a moderately successful and happy team than be massively successful on my own.'

- **Husband**. 'Even though we've only been married a year, I realise that the "honeymoon period" will fade and that a marriage can require effort. I must never let my career get so busy that I neglect the relationship that I hope will sustain me for the rest of my life.'

- **Health**. 'I can't be doing without eating healthily and exercising. Whatever my workload, I must ensure that I can swim a couple of times a week and look after myself.'

- **Fairness**. 'Treating everyone I meet with respect and receiving respect from them is a must-have in my life. I've had to put up with some rubbish from clients in recent years, but no longer! If people aren't good for how I feel, I will find ways to remove them from my life.'

My last words on values are that it *almost* goes without saying that you have to be honest with yourself. Just as your vision needs to reflect your authentic desires in life, your values must stand for how *you* want to live – and not how you think you should be living. Given that no one else need ever see your list of values, the only person you'd deceive is yourself. So before we move on, look at your values statements and ask yourself:

- Is every one of the values that you have chosen deeply important to you?

- Are you sure that you're not creating a set of values that reflects what your parents or partner, friends, colleagues, or anyone else might deem appropriate?

- Do you feel good when you look at the list and feel that you've captured the person you would like to be?

If you answer 'no' to any of those questions, be careful that you're not trying to impose values on yourself that don't really reflect what would make you happy and confident. We all carry baggage with us from our upbringing, and the messages that we hear from society, organised religion, the media, our peer groups, and so on. So work on your values until you can look at them and feel happy that they represent the life you genuinely want to live.

"Above all be true to yourself, and if you cannot put your heart into it, take yourself out of it."

Hardy D. Jackson, author

A word of advice: Avoid the lure of the quick-fix

You may be thinking: vision and values?!? Maybe you picked up this book wanting to feel more confident in a couple of areas of your life, such as public speaking or dating, being a parent or socialising. And maybe now you've skipped the vision and values stuff and are heading straight to setting goals.

Of course that's your prerogative. Let's face it: most of us want a quick-fix. A miracle diet, an overnight relationship makeover, instant confidence. We like immediate, easy, painless results – and yes, you'll find other books or experts saying you can get confidence in a jiffy. But I'm sharing with you an approach that will give you the *best* confidence. You get out of this book what you put in.

The tools and techniques in this book work. They don't work without effort on your part. *But they work.* Decades of research by eminent scientists from around the world tell us the best ways to set goals and boost our confidence. Trust me – I'm a psychologist!

Tackling an isolated area or two of your life may seem like an attractive shortcut. But every aspect of your life is interconnected. Start working on a few areas of your life and you may discover there are opportunities to grow and develop in other areas of your life too. Only when you consider your life as a whole can you spot the best ways to invest your time and effort. And your path to your new, more confident whole life begins by considering your long-term vision and the values you hold dear.

So, can you spare the time to ponder your vision and values?

You can't be in the game without a goal

Great, you have your vision and values. You'll be pleased to hear that those are two of the hardest exercises to do in this book. If you've got those worked out, the rest should be a piece of cake!

Your vision is an exciting but broad picture of where you want to get to and what you want to achieve. You probably have some pretty big aspirations in your vision – you're selling yourself short if your vision isn't at least a little daunting. But how do you get there? Your values guide the big decisions in your life, but knowing that you want to live honestly and be successful, or to have fun with your family, doesn't tell you the steps you need to take to achieve your vision either. So how do you work out the steps you need to take?

To explain, let's consider that holiday you booked (back on page 74). Thinking about where you're going on holiday should make the excitement bubble up inside you. But to get ready for it, you need to make a list of tasks to complete. Get your holiday clothes out of storage and borrow a bigger suitcase from a friend. Drop off your favourite outfit at the dry cleaner. Dig out your passport. Buy a new pair of sunglasses and some Factor 15.

In the same way, you need to create specific goals and plans to achieve your vision. And until you achieve it, your vision motivates you to keep forging ahead, ticking the items off your goals and plans.

SPOT the goal

There's a lot of powerful psychology to setting effective goals. Study after study shows that people are more successful at following through on their goals when they consider exactly when and where and how they can work on them. All you need to do is remember the letters SPOT.

Stretching and significant

S is for stretching and significant. OK, I cheated a little – there should be two 'S's. But your goal has to be both challenging and worthwhile.

Your goal has to be at least ambitious enough for you to need to push yourself to achieve it. Research shows that people often underestimate their ability. You're probably better than you think you are. So set yourself a goal that will stretch and challenge you. If you do that, you may surprise yourself as to what you can achieve.

But aim to stretch, not snap. Just as an elastic band has a point at which it stops stretching and simply snaps, you don't want to set yourself a goal that is so out-of-this-world that you couldn't possibly achieve it. A bit of stretch is more motivating than an easily attainable goal. But an unrealistic and entirely unattainable goal will only make you feel frustrated and fed up. So stretch, but don't snap.

The second 'S' refers to significance. Your goal has to be impor-tant, appealing, alluring. You have to want it. Badly. If your goal isn't exciting and a big deal, you could end up getting distracted. Sure, it would be nice to learn another language, but do you want to do it because you *should* or because you honestly love the idea and can't wait to fly off and try your new language skills? Yes, it would be cool to get that promotion, but is that because your other half is pressurising you or because you can't wait to take on more responsibility? Make sure you choose goals that make you want to jump up and down because *you* want them so much.

Positive

Imagine for a moment that you're on a diet and someone says to you: 'Don't eat any chocolate, don't think about the sound it makes as you break a piece off or the smell as you pop it into your mouth. And definitely don't think about the taste as it melts on your tongue and oozes down your throat.' What do you think you're going to end up thinking and obsessing about, craving and drooling over? Chocolate, of course.

When you set a goal, you get what you focus on. Set yourself a negative goal such as 'I want to worry less' and your mind focuses on the 'worry'. You end up worrying more. Tell yourself 'I don't want to embarrass myself in meetings' and your mind latches on to the word 'embarrass' – you end up feeling more self-conscious than before. Goals that contain 'don't' or 'not' or 'less' are self-defeating. Better then to set yourself positive goals such as 'I want to think more optimistically' or 'I want to be a confident participant in meetings'.

Research backs all of this up too. Laboratory studies show that people who set positive goals about what they want are more likely to achieve them than people who set negative goals about what they want to avoid.

You get the point. So how can you phrase your goals in terms of what you want to develop, gain, or hone?

Observable

Say you set yourself a goal to 'get better at socialising at parties'. How would you know when you've achieved it? Would talking to 20 new people get you the tick in the box? How about if you talk to only 10, 6 or 1 new person?

For a goal to be effective, it should be observable to other people whether you've reached it or not. Unless you quantify your goal, you won't know when to give yourself a pat on the back for achieving it. Your goal should be specific and obvious enough that an impartial onlooker could nod and say 'yes, you've achieved your goal' or, with a shake of the head, say 'no, not yet'.

Contrast these observable (and effective) versus opaque (and ineffective) goals:

Observable versus opaque goals

Observable goals	Opaque goals
'I will speak up at least three times during team meetings.'	'I want to get noticed during team meetings.'
'I want to get the name of my business mentioned in a national newspaper.'	'I want to be a famous entrepreneur.'
'I will be more adventurous by trying a small, new experience daily.'	'I want to be more adventurous with my choices in life.'
'I will call my parents once a week for at least a 10-minute chat.'	'I must make more of an effort with my parents.'

Timed

So you want to ask for that pay rise, overcome your fear of public speaking, find a hot date. Or stand up to someone, volunteer for charity work, set up your own business. The question is: when?

Deadlines are motivating. If you make a promise that you'll do something by a certain date, that's a much bigger commitment than saying 'you'll get round to it'. A deadline acts as a powerful reminder, a mental kick in the backside.

But set yourself too distant a deadline – 'I'll get that pay rise by the year 2025' – and you may as well not have one. On the other hand, aim to achieve it by next month and you may be putting yourself under too much time pressure. So choose a date for the completion of your goal that is challenging yet realistic. Choose a date that compels you to take action today, but not one that will drive you crazy with worry about how you're going to get it done in time.

Even better, if you can pick a significant deadline for it. Perhaps by your next birthday, wedding anniversary, Christmas, Hanukkah, date of the next England away-game, or anything else that will stick in your mind until you have achieved your goal.

You may be wondering: 'But what if I fail to achieve the goal by the allotted deadline? Wouldn't it be better to allow a bit of extra time to make doubly sure I can achieve my goal in time?' The answer's no. A big N-O. Sure, if you're delivering a project at work or promising to help a friend out by a certain date, you need to keep your promises. But when it comes to taking action in pursuit of your personal goals, a goal that compels you to take action sooner trumps a goal that allows you to take action later. Better to have achieved 80 to 90 per cent of your goal by the deadline than to have such a distant deadline that you can keep putting off action. Go on, give yourself a testing timeframe.

Here's the bit where you get involved

OK, I've talked enough about setting effective goals. I'm sure you get the idea. SPOT – that's simple enough, right? But as I've mentioned before (and will mention again), you get the biggest benefits from this book by taking action and not just reading.

So what are your goals? How can you translate that broad picture of your amazing future into a set of concrete goals?

Take Action: What do you really, really want?

Your vision is an inspiring picture of the future you would like to achieve. Your values are a set of guidelines on how you should behave to feel strong and confident.

To translate your vision and values into a set of goals, consider: what are the three things you want most from your vision and values? Write these down by completing the sentence 'I want ...' three times.

Of course, you may have more than three goals. But for now let's stick with three. When you're starting out on the path to a more confident life, you are better off having a small number of goals. If you have too many goals, you could end up spreading your efforts too thinly. When you've achieved or made significant progress on these initial three goals, you can always come back to your vision and add further new goals.

Next, take each of your three statements and rewrite it as a SPOT goal. Remember to make it Stretching and significant, Positive, Observable and Timed.

If they can do it ...

Patrick is a 37-year-old successful graphic designer working in the marketing department of an international healthcare company. He enjoys the creative aspects of his job but works with large teams on enormous projects, which means that he only gets to work on a tiny part of the overall puzzle. He has been feeling for some time that he is a cog in a huge machine and realises he needs to change something to avoid feeling unfulfilled in his work for the rest of his life.

He completes the vision and values exercises and decides that he would love to set up his own graphic design agency. His vision sees him at the heart of a small business, with a few enthusiastic staff working for him. And one of his core values is to have total control over his work. He would be able to pursue smaller projects that he could work on in their entirety rather than just fragments of larger ones.

To help him retain his focus, he turns his vision into a SPOT goal.

- **Stretching and significant**. 'I want to set up my own business and be able to choose the kinds of projects I do.' This goal feels pretty stretching for him because he has never worked for himself; he needs to learn about the administrative side of running a business. But it's significant too as he really longs to work on smaller projects that he can manage from beginning to end.

- **Positive**. 'I want to earn enough money to pay my bills and allow me to have at least two holidays a year.' He phrases his goal in terms of what he wants rather than what he wants to avoid (e.g. 'I don't want to have to worry about money').

- **Observable**. 'I will start to look for new clients by researching small companies that may need the services of a freelance graphic designer – I will call 10 companies a day.' His goal is clearly observable as an impartial onlooker could simply count the number of potential clients that he calls every day.

- **Timed**. 'I will be working for myself in six months' time.' Because he doesn't know everything he needs to know about running a business, he gives himself six months to research what he needs to do. By giving himself a deadline, he knows he will have to get a move on straightaway.

The power of the pen

You've got a vision, values and a set of goals now, right? If you haven't, please consider putting pen to paper or fingers on keyboard to capture the thoughts and dreams you have running around in your head. If you want to change your life and grow in confidence, then put your confidence in me. Trust me when I say you need to write up your vision, values, and goals before moving on.

There's a piece of research that is often written about in self-improvement books and I'll repeat it for you here. Back in the 1950s, a bunch of researchers asked Harvard University graduates about their goals. As you might expect, most of these fresh-faced kids had goals. But only 3 per cent of them actually wrote their goals down. Fast-forward 30 years to a follow-up survey and guess what? The 3 per cent had accumulated as much wealth as the other 97 per cent put together.

I suspect that the story is just an urban myth that has been repeated and repeated over the years. But the fact that it remains such a popular story hints at the power of writing stuff down.

Thankfully, there is also genuine science supporting the importance of capturing our goals in writing. Research psychologists Delia Cioffi and Randy Garner conducted a study in which they stopped students who were strolling around on campus; the psychologists asked them if they would be willing to volunteer to take part in an education programme about AIDS in local schools. Half of the students were asked to sign a form saying that they would take part; the other half merely read a nearly identical form and agreed verbally that they would take part. A few days later, the students who had signed a simple form were three times more likely to turn up than the students who had merely read the form.

Let's think about that. *Three times* more likely. That's a big, big deal. Writing goals down really does have a special power over us. It helps to make our thoughts more real. We can't dismiss them as easily. We help ourselves to succeed. So do you want to triple your chances of success?

Baby steps for big results

Great, you've got goals. And you've put them somewhere prominent to remind yourself of your commitments. What next?

I know it's a cliché to say that a journey of a thousand miles begins with a single step. But just because it has been said many times does not make it any less true.

Imagine that your goal is to run a marathon in a year's time. You'd have to be fairly daft to think that you could wake up on the morning of the race, put on your training shoes and run 26 miles. So how would you get ready for it? Of course, you'd start off by doing a short run. Or maybe a brisk walk if you're really out of shape. After a few weeks, you'd be running a mile. A month later, you'd be running a few miles. And then 10 miles, 11, 12, 13, and more.

You will achieve your goals and develop an abundance of confidence in exactly the same way. Sure, we'd all love to have instant results, but that's daydreaming, not reality. Confident people break their goals down into a series of individual actions that allow them, step-by-step, to achieve their goals.

If your ultimate goal is to move into a dramatically different career, you may need to build up certain skills, pick up particular experience, and make the right contacts. You may need to go on a course, sit an exam, gain a qualification or two as well.

If part of your vision is to buy a house in the countryside where you can live a more peaceful life, you may need to put aside money every month towards it. You may need to research potential areas to live, and look at how you would make a living if you were to move. If you have a partner and children, you would have to consider their needs too.

Whatever your goal, make a list of all the actions you need to take to move forward. Start by writing down every action that comes to mind. Treat it as a solo brainstorm. Scribble every action, big and small, that comes to mind. Don't concern yourself about what order you'd need to do them in or when you're going to get the time to fit it all in.

Make an exhaustive list. Finally, look at your list of actions and pick one out that you can do today. If you could do several of them, pick the one you like the look of most. Then do it. Yes, right now. Take that first step towards your vision and goals. Put the book down and *do*, not read.

Action before confidence

Congratulations if you put the book down and did something – if you managed to take that first action. You're part of an elite minority of people who actually have more self-belief than they might have thought.

But don't beat yourself up if you read the last section and carried on reading to this section. You may be thinking that I've sprung it a bit suddenly on you. Perhaps you were hoping there'd be a few more exercises to help you build up your confidence before you actually had to *do* anything.

The truth is that setting goals and listing actions are a great start – but they aren't enough. Your confidence grows as a result of your actions, not intentions. Lots of people have good intentions. How many times have you heard friends saying 'I wish I could lose weight' or 'I need to get a new job' or 'I wish I could give up smoking' or 'I'd love to run my own business' or the many other deeds people *intend* to do? But unless an intention is turned into an action, it's really only a thought in someone's head (or words on a sheet of paper).

People sometimes wait to 'feel confident' before taking action. But that isn't how it works, I'm afraid. Action precedes confidence – not the other way around. Taking action will make you feel confident. Wait to feel more confident before taking action and it will probably never come.

Remember the notion that what we *do, think,* and *feel* are interlinked. As it happens, most people find it harder to change how they feel than to change how they behave. So avoid waiting around for the confidence to arrive from nowhere, because it won't.

Back in Chapter 1, I defined confidence as 'the ability to take appropriate and effective action, however challenging it may feel at the time'. Most people feel a little scared when they take on new challenges. But you can kill those anxious feelings by taking action. Take even a small action and you feel a little more confident. Take another action and that feeling of confidence swells still further. Do it again and again and your initial successes pave the way for larger ones. Make no mistake: you may not be confident when you start, but you have to start to be confident.

"Success seems to be connected with action.
Successful people keep moving."

Conrad Hilton Sr, hotelier

That first action

Kick off with even the tiniest action and you may find that it generates its own momentum. If a task is daunting, tell yourself that you will do it for five minutes today. Come on, a mere five minutes. There are 24 hours in the day and all you need to commit right now is one-twelfth of one hour. That still leaves you with 287 other twelfths-of-an-hour to do whatever else you feel like doing!

If you're on the lookout for a new job, dig out your old CV and scribble some notes on the bits you'll change. Spend a few minutes on it today and your subconscious mind can work on it overnight. If you want to get into better physical shape, at least change into your workout clothes and go for a brisk walk today if you can't face the gym until tomorrow. Even a few minutes of action today is better than nothing until tomorrow.

The point is simply *to begin*. You will feel better about your task and yourself immediately. Who knows? You might even enjoy it and find yourself doing it for another five minutes.

But even if you only last that first five minutes, congratulate yourself. Smiling is free, so give yourself a big smile. And tell yourself – perhaps quietly in your head if you're surrounded by people – how proud you are that you have followed through with your first action towards achieving your goals. When I'm at my desk and I feel good about what I've achieved, I sometimes do whoop and clap or get up and do a funky dance. You may think that's stupid, but hell, it makes me feel good!

Over to you

What could *you* do right now? Rather than reading on to the next section of this book, what could you do right now – for just five minutes? Whether you're looking for more confidence in your personal or professional life, spend just a few minutes working towards your goals. Put the book down and *do something*. Make a list, pick up the phone, send an email, go for a walk, research jobs online, throw out the junk food, or whatever else will help you to move you closer to your goals. Even the tiniest little action will get the ball rolling. You'll feel better, brighter, more confident with just one action. Go on, give it a go!

"A good plan vigorously executed right now is far better than a perfect plan executed next week."

George S. Patton, US General

Building momentum

They say that the devil is in the detail. And I think the saying means that if you overlook some of the details of a plan, things could all go horribly wrong.

I prefer to say that the angel is in the detail. Because when it comes to turning your intentions into reality, thinking through your actions in more detail means you will be more ready to succeed.

Psychologists make a distinction between plain old intentions and *implementation* intentions. We class the two separately because we know from decades of research and many studies that people who plan at the implementation level are much more likely to carry out their intentions.

An implementation intention is the fleshed-out version of the actions you listed to achieve your goal. It is detailed in terms of exactly what you will do, who else might be involved, where it will happen, and when it will happen.

Say you want to get in shape and have set yourself a goal to do 20 push-ups and 40 sit-ups every day. Rather than just promise you're going to do it every day, you can help yourself to succeed by thinking through exactly how you will make it happen. Will you do it in the morning by dropping to the floor right next to your bed? How about in the kitchen while the kettle is boiling for your first cup of coffee for the day? Or in the evening in front of the television while you're watching your favourite show?

Honestly, taking that little extra time to think through the details of your plan can make all the difference. Here's the science bit. Professors Peter Gollwitzer and Veronika Brandstätter studied a group of students who had to write an essay on how they spent Christmas Eve. But the twist was that the students had to submit their assignments on 26 December. As you can imagine, only a third of the students managed to get their papers in on time. But the researchers had also asked a second group of students to create a specific, observable, and timed outcome, thinking about both when *and* where they intended to write their reports. A massive 75 per cent of the students in this group managed to get their assignments in on time.

The lesson is clear. If you want to double your chances of achieving your goals, take a few extra moments to think about not only the 'what' but also the 'when', 'where', and 'how'. And a handy way to turn your common-variety intentions into super-sexy implementation intentions is to draw up a little table:

Action plan

1 What?	2 How exactly?	3 Who is involved?	4 Where?	5 When?
Action 1				
Action 2				
Action 3 ...				

If they can do it ...

David, 33, is trying to get out of debt. Having just proposed to his girlfriend Louisa, he has set himself a SPOT goal: to pay off £10,000 of his debts within the next two years. Here are a few of his actions.

1 What?	2 How exactly?	3 Who is involved?	4 Where?	5 When?
Research ways to pay off my debts.	Phone banks to see if I can get a better interest rate on the mortgage.	Just me.	I'll set up a bedroom office so I don't get disturbed by Louisa watching TV in the lounge.	A week on Monday – when I have the day off work.
More research.	Get advice from Jason on whether I should get a financial adviser.	Jason – I think he has a good financial adviser.	At home.	When Louisa and I are meeting him and his wife for dinner in two weeks' time.
More research.	Look online to see if I can get a better deal on my credit cards.	Rod at work is a whiz at finding things online.	On my work computer.	Tomorrow – if Rod can spare 20 minutes to help.
Spend less money.	Calculate a budget to figure out exactly how much I need to get by on a weekly basis.	Me and Louisa.	At home.	This weekend when Louisa is off work.

Fill up your table by working through these five steps:

1 Copy your individual actions into the left-hand column.

2 Think about how that action would look if you had to tell a 12-year-old child to do it for you. You'd need to be a lot more specific. While in column 1 you could say 'Look for a new job', in column 2 you'd have to go into detail: 'Send emails to ex-colleagues and acquaintances to see if they have vacancies for a teaching assistant.'

3 Ask yourself if someone else could help you complete your action. For example, if I wanted to lose weight, I know that a friend has just hired a personal trainer so I'd ask my friend for his opinions on whether I should get one too. We need all the help we can get, so if you know someone who could offer support or advice, take it.

4 Consider if your action would be best performed in any particular location. Do you need to find an Ashram for your yoga class, a library to read up on new techniques to use in your job, an internet café to research potential new employers online, a swanky restaurant to entertain your friends?

5 Finally, give yourself a deadline for the action. While your overall goal may have a deadline of many weeks or months, your individual actions should probably have deadlines of days, or a couple of weeks at most. Put actions on the back-burner and you risk leaving them there for ever.

Congratulations. You now have a concrete plan of action. Put it somewhere you'll see it daily. Stick a copy on your fridge. Or photocopy it and put multiple copies around your home or workplace.

Don't shove it in a drawer. And if you work through your actions one by one, you will soon be reaping the benefits of a more confident, new you.

If tomorrow never comes

If confidence is about taking action in spite of how you may feel, procrastination is its evil nemesis. Procrastination is about avoiding immediate action because of how you feel. Both confidence and procrastination fuel the *do, think, feel* cycle. Confident actions lead to confident beliefs and confident feelings. Postponing action leads to beliefs that you can't do it and looming fears that you will never do it. Avoidance leads to a vicious circle: the more you avoid, the more you want to avoid.

Some people put off making decisions and taking action because they want to feel more certain that their decisions will be the 'right' ones. Especially when it comes to making the big decisions in life, they have a 'wait and see' attitude, hoping the perfect plan or right moment will come along. But often waiting provides only a false sense of security – when it comes to making life decisions, we can't ever know that we've made the 'right' choices. Few decisions in life are clear-cut enough for one choice to leap out as being unambiguously better than the other choices you have. And if you wait too long, you will end up missing opportunities. That job offer won't stay open for ever. That person you're attracted to could end up going out with someone else. That house you want to buy could get snapped up by another buyer.

If you find yourself putting action off until tomorrow again and again, you're not alone. Surveys show that around one in five people consider themselves not only to be procrastinators but *chronic* procrastinators. Thankfully, there is a technique to shift how you feel and give you an extra little push to act.

Confidence Booster: Rut-busting

There is no magic wand I can wave to make you do anything. *You* are the only one who can make yourself begin what you need to do. But here's a simple technique to pile the pressure on you just that little bit more.

Time to get your trusty journal or notepad out. If you want to say goodbye to your delaying tactics, write down the answers to these questions the next time you are dallying over a task:

- What are the *advantages* of starting this right now?

- What are the *disadvantages* of leaving this till later?

- What *excuses* are you using to avoid doing this right now?

- What do you have to *lose*?

- What *reward* can you give yourself for starting this?

If they can do it …

Julia is a 45-year-old photographer. She has been invited to a get-together of some of her old friends. But she is worried that her friends could be making more money, might be married and living in big houses, and so on. But by working through the rut-busting technique, she realises that:

- the *advantage* of going is that she would catch up with friends she has not seen in years and perhaps re-establish a few friendships

- the *disadvantage* of not going is that she would not see them for many years and rob herself of the opportunity to reinstate old friendships

- her *excuse* is that she doesn't feel she measures up against their happier and more successful lives

- she has nothing to *lose*: in the worst-case scenario, she could leave early and it would only waste two hours of a single evening

- as an *incentive* to go, she decides to buy a new dress that she could wear again at other events.

Rather than wait for circumstances to change and confidence to fall in your lap (which rarely happens), you can bring about change in your life. You can grasp the confidence you want. But remember that this is not a book to read and set aside. You can grow your confidence only if you participate, work through the exercises, do the thinking, and take that first step. So what are the advantages of starting your first action right now?

Remember that confidence is about taking action in spite of the doubts you may have or the nervousness you feel. You will feel more confident once you've taken action. You'll feel relieved and proud. You may even sleep better for it – so do it now.

ONWARDS AND UPWARDS

- ▪ You can feel more in control and confident about your life by creating a vision of what you would like to have in your life. If life is a journey, then your vision is a picture of your destination.

- ▪ Think about your strengths, the skills you have and enjoy using. Incorporate these into your vision and help yourself to thrive.

- ▪ To create your vision, imagine a celebratory party thrown in your honour, say five or ten years in the future. What would you like to have going on in your life by then?

- ▪ Confident people know their values – the set of principles or guidelines by which they want to live their lives. If you understand your values, you can make more confident choices about what to invest your time and energy into and what to turn down.

- ▪ There's a lot of science behind effective goal setting, and it shows two things. First, that you can help yourself to achieve goals if you make plans as to when and how you will take action. Second, that you should write your goals and plans down.

- ▪ And don't forget to make your goals stretching and significant, positive, observable, and timed (SPOT).

- ▪ Remember that your confidence grows as a result of your actions. Avoid waiting until you feel more confident before you take action. Jump in and *do* something to feel more confident.

Drawing on your resources

"Few men during their lifetime come anywhere near exhausting the resources dwelling in them."

Richard Evelyn Byrd, polar explorer

In this chapter you will ...

■ identify the unique resources that allow you to recharge your confidence batteries

■ consider how people in your life can support, encourage, and advise you

■ make a list of your past accomplishments and successes to remind you of all that you have achieved and all that you can still achieve in the future

■ discover the skill of mindfulness as a way of banishing worry

■ learn – or more likely remind yourself of – the importance of looking after both body and mind

■ appreciate the best times of day for you to take on challenging activities.

You can look forward to having some great, confidence-filled days. As you make progress towards your goals, you are certain to achieve more and feel stronger than you have before. However, your mood and confidence may still ebb and flow from day to day. A run of good days may be punctuated by the occasional bad one. Perhaps you have an argument with someone at work, receive a critical comment from someone, or find that your computer has deleted an important file. We all experience problems, conflicts, and nuisances that can leave us feeling anything from angry and wanting to scream to deflated or downright sad.

Fortunately we all have personal sources of strength that we can draw upon to boost our mood and replenish our confidence. Rather than let your feelings get the better of you, you can take action to restore your confidence. By reviewing thoroughly the full range of resources at your disposal, you can recharge your batteries at will. Learn to restore and maintain your confidence in even the toughest of times.

You are one of a kind

Different people draw their strength from different sources. When I have a bad day, I go to the gym and throw weights around. My better half bakes muffins. A good friend shoves himself under the bonnet of a classic car with an oily rag. A client of mine builds her own computers.

What might your resources include? A few of your resources such as your closest friends or most cherished possessions may be sources of strength that are common to many people. But you may have ones that are unique to you too. Consider:

- engaging in activities such as exercise, cooking, having a hot bath, singing
- focusing on your spirituality or faith
- immersing yourself in art or music
- spending time with people
- recollecting positive experiences from the past
- visiting special places
- reading books, inspirational quotations, or stories about historical figures.

You may have a favourite few resources that you habitually draw upon. Perhaps you immerse yourself in a 'boxercise' or Pilates class, press play on your favourite DVD, rustle up a gourmet meal. Maybe you ease into a hot bath lit by scented candles, shoot aliens in an online computer game, or pick up the phone to a friend.

But it's important not to rely on the same old resources all of the time. Because some resources can help you feel good in different ways or at different times. The point of this next exercise is to figure out the full range of rituals, activities, and other sources of strength that you could use. When you feel battered or down, what are the many different and unique ways you could help yourself to recover?

Take Action: Tapping your reserves of confidence

Write down the ways in which you help yourself to feel better or unwind. Simply take the phrase 'I feel good when I ...' and complete it as many times as you can. Don't discount any of the ideas that pop into your head. And the more specific you can be, the more you help yourself to feel better when you're not feeling at your best.

You may wish to complete this exercise over several days or even weeks. If you leave it to one side for a while, you may find that other ideas gradually percolate through from your subconscious.

Once you've completed your list, consider which are constructive ways to feel better about yourself and which are less so. For example, even though having *one* scoop of ice cream may be a great way to unwind, does having *three* scoops every night still constitute a productive way to feel better?

Keep and treasure this list as a little catalogue of the ways in which you can manage your emotions and maintain your confidence.

Your turn. This will take you mere seconds to begin drawing up your list of resources. Grab a pen and complete these three phrases to begin with.

■ I feel good when I ....

....

■ I feel good when I ....

....

■ I feel good when I ....

....

If they can do it …

Adam, 46, is a freelance television producer who recently got divorced. He loves his job but finds the ups and downs of his work very demanding. When he's between contracts, he worries about earning enough to pay the bills. When he is working, he puts in long hours and has to deal with the demands of picky executive producers and diva-like actors. To help him cope with both his work stress and the scary prospect of meeting new people and dating again, he writes a list of his resources, completing the phrase 'I feel good when I …' Here are the first 10 items that he thinks of:

- … spend time with my two children – especially playing football in the garden, helping them with their homework or teaching them to cook us a meal.

- … listen to music – particularly Madeleine Peyroux when I need to calm down. And tracks like 'Supermassive black hole' by Muse and 'I predict a riot' by Kaiser Chiefs when I need more energy.

- … cycle through the park – especially late evenings when the park is dark and quiet.

- … laugh while watching *The Simpsons* and *Family Guy* DVDs.

- … grind coffee beans and make a fresh pot of coffee. Although when I'm away from home, a double shot of extra-hot latte does the job too!

- … do 30 press-ups in the morning.

- … talk things over with Chris. Even if it's only a quick conversation by telephone or instant message, I can rely on him to talk some sense into me when I'm being daft.

- … phone Dad and 'talk' to the dogs. Something about hearing them barking in the background makes me grin like crazy.

- … read dark thrillers by Kathy Reichs and Lee Child but also quick reads by James Patterson, David Baldacci, or anyone who writes like them.

- … discuss the latest match results with anyone who has an opinion.

Once you have your list of resources, be sure to draw upon them regularly. Create time for yourself to use them – perhaps first thing in the morning, straight after you get home from work or last thing at night. Sure, you may have a lot of work on or responsibilities at home that make it a struggle to find the time. But what about your responsibility to yourself?

Even if it's only a 10-minute break you can claw out for yourself in the middle of a busy day, make it a habit to replenish your energy and confidence on a daily basis. Do it and you can rest assured that you can get over pretty much whatever jagged reality throws at you.

With a little help from our friends

The human race is innately sociable. We need social interaction. Even the most self-sufficient of individuals reaps benefits from spending time with other people. So why take the journey to greater confidence alone? Best friends, parents, relatives, a teacher from school, colleagues from work, an ex-boss, mentors, a neighbour or two – seek out people who can provide you with encouragement, support, advice, and sympathy. Enlist them as accomplices in helping you to succeed.

Share your goals and plans to help yourself to succeed. For starters, by making a promise in front of people you care about, you won't want to let them down.

But before you pick up the phone, type out an email, or drop by to visit, consider that different people are suited to different forms of support. While my own mother is a great source of optimism and unconditional love, I know that she's not best suited to telling me when I'm going wrong or being ridiculous. Equally, while one of my ex-bosses has a sharp and insightful mind when it comes to telling me how to get out of a jam, he's not the kind of person who is terribly good at giving positive strokes.

Who could remind you of your commitments and challenge you when you're in danger of faltering? Who could provide you with compassion and commiserations when you're feeling down? And who could you turn to for advice about an impasse with a colleague, a decision in your career, or a dilemma in your love life?

Whoever you approach, avoid seeking the advice of people who will treat the discussion as an opportunity to tell you where you're going wrong and what you should do. Look for people who will listen and help you to come to your own decision. When you're trying to build your self-confidence, you need people to prompt and support you, not take responsibility for your decisions and make you become dependent on them.

"Friendship makes prosperity more shining and lessens adversity by dividing and sharing it."

Cicero, Roman philosopher

Frenemies and friends

Apparently, socialite and heiress Paris Hilton uses the word 'frenemy' to refer to the friend-enemies that surround her. In a surprisingly sharp way, she realises that not all of the people who besiege her may truly have her best interests at heart.

Not all of the people that surround you may be equally good for your confidence. If people treat you a certain way, you will come to believe that you are that way – and behave like it too. If you spend time with positive people who encourage you, you will feel more confident about yourself. If you allow yourself to be plagued by negative people who put you down, your confidence is likely to spiral downwards too.

Now that may sound obvious. But have you ever considered what to do with the so-called friends and acquaintances that might not be so good for you? Naturally, you want to be liked by everyone. But if certain people undermine your confidence, or drain your enthusiasm and energy, you may need to take a stand. If you are constantly investing more in particular relationships than you get back, consider reducing dramatically the time you spend with them. If any relationships are especially toxic, get rid of them entirely. No matter what your past history with them, you need to look after yourself and assert your right to a more confident life.

But just as bad people can sap your confidence, the right people can boost it. A big part of how we behave is determined by how we see others behaving around us. So consider which of your acquaintances are good for your confidence and could help you achieve your goals. If you want to get better at standing up to bossy colleagues, make sure to lunch with a friend who's already great at it. If you're trying to study more diligently, spend a bit more time with your more bookish friends. Share your goals with like-minded people and allow them to support you. Confidence can be contagious – who would you like to infect you?

Take Action: Choosing your comrades with care

Psychologists, sociologists and even economists have been gathering evidence for several decades that the people we surround ourselves with can have a material impact on our behaviour and well-being. Hang out with smokers and of course you'll have a harder time quitting cigarettes. Keep meeting up with keen sports fans and naturally you will end up watching more matches. Plus research by the University of Missouri found that groups of friends who talked excessively about their problems and worries were more prone to depression and anxiety. It stands to reason then that if you spend more time with supportive, encouraging people, some of it will rub off on you too.

For this exercise, draw two lines down a sheet of paper to divide it into three. Write the letters 'A', 'B', and 'C' across the top.

A	B	C

Now bring to mind the names of your friends (go through your address book or look at who you send emails to if it helps you to remember who you know) to populate each of the three categories as follows:

- **A.** Your most supportive, positive, and encouraging friends. These friends are the people who are most interested in your life, what you're up to, and how you're feeling. You'll be able to spot these people because you always feel good after you've seen them. They look after you. They ask about what you've been up to; they show genuine delight when you do well and concern when you don't. They remember what your interests and priorities are. When they do talk about themselves, they are positive, upbeat, and optimistic. You may not necessarily see these people that often, but when you do, you always feel cherished by them and nourished by your time together.

- **B.** Friends who are quite supportive and interested in your well-being. These friends are somewhere between the A friends and your C friends, which I describe next.

- **C.** Other people who support you the least. You may see these people quite a lot and sometimes have fun with them. But deep-down you probably know that they aren't necessarily the best people for you to be with. They probably don't ask very many questions about your life – they probably talk more about themselves than listen to you. Or they may be prone to negative thinking, pessimism, or bitching about other people. These are probably friends that you hang out with as opposed to close friends or people who are good for you. Especially if your confidence is at all fragile, you probably know that there are better people for you to be around.

Now look at your three lists. Sure, you may have fun with your C friends, but are they ultimately good for helping you to grow and expand your horizons? If you want to feel more encouraged and confident, then look for ways to spend more time with your A friends. I'm not suggesting that you do away entirely with your C friends, only that you consider how you allocate the limited time you have for socialising. Now write down three actions you will take within the next week that will help you to surround yourself with the right kind of caring, affirming, confidence-boosting friends.

Helping our home and work spaces to help us

Say you want to lose weight. We all know that willpower is something that comes and goes for us all. But an immediate action you can take is to banish all sugary and fatty snacks from the cupboard. Because deep-down you know that, in a moment of weakness, you may well succumb to that chocolate bar or packet of biscuits.

Changing your life takes a bit of effort. Sometimes you can help yourself not by changing your behaviour but by changing your environment. If you want to boost your confidence about your body, then surrounding yourself with magazines of air-brushed supermodels isn't going to help you feel good about yourself. Throw out those glossy magazines. If you're trying to do more exercise, then having your gym kit stuffed at the back of your wardrobe doesn't help you when you have to dig it out every time. Put your favourite gym outfit in plain sight so you see it the moment you come home from work to remind yourself it's gym o'clock.

The same goes for work as well as home. If you get distracted by what's going on outside your window when you should be working at your desk, why not move your desk so you face a blank wall? If you waste a lot of time chatting to the colleague who sits opposite you, why not build a pile of books between you so you can't make eye contact as easily?

Your environment is yours to shape. Whether it's to remove stuff that could sabotage your goals or introduce new things into it, consider the changes you could make. Put a favourite photo of yourself on your fridge to remind you not to reach for that unhealthy snack. Put a sticky note on the inside of your front door to remind you to smile and think positively before you leave the house. Buy an extension cable for your computer if studying with the kids in the same room is distracting. Anything to help you attain your goals.

Over to you

To give yourself the best shot at achieving your goals, get a pen right now and write down three things you will do today to change your environment.

- I will ....

- I will ....

- I will ....

Investing in a confidence bank

The producers of a major TV dance show asked me for help recently – strictly speaking, I can't mention its name. Three of the celebrities on the show felt they were cracking under the pressure of the live shows. Two of the celebrities were famous performers; one was a glamorous lingerie model. And to help them conquer their nerves, I suggested this next exercise.

Do you smile when you look through an album of old photos? Get taken back to a perfect moment when you hear a favourite song? Laugh with old friends or colleagues about when you lived or studied or worked together? If you do, you've already experienced the power of *reminiscence*.

Reminding yourself of past successes and happy times is an intoxicatingly powerful tool for fuelling your mood and confidence in a few moments. Researcher Fred Bryant at the University of Chicago found that as little as 10 minutes of reminiscing was enough to have a significant impact on how people felt.

It's a versatile tool too. You can use it to restore your confidence after a rough day, a rejection, an argument, or whatever else has happened. Or you can use it to prepare yourself for a daunting challenge, a driving test, your first day in a new job, a big date.

Many people underestimate the scale of their past successes and emotional highpoints. They downplay or take for granted what they have accomplished or experienced. But you shouldn't! Jogging your memory about all you have done so far is a great way to remind yourself that you are more resilient than you may sometimes feel. Looking at your past, you will see that you are still capable of so much more in the present and future. You can tell yourself: 'I've done all this so far, I can do even more now.' This next exercise gets you to ponder the FACTs of life.

Take Action: Considering the FACTs of life

This exercise is about bringing to mind all of your Feats, Achievements, Challenges overcome, and Triumphs. Take a sheet of paper and write down every success you can think of. If in doubt, write it down. You can edit the list later.

Consider it an autobiography of what you've done and like about yourself. Use the broadest definition of the word 'success' possible. Some of your successes may be grand in scope; others may be smaller and more personal. Think about all of the different areas of your life including your financial and work success, family and friends, education, problems in life you overcame, and changes or hardships you have coped with. Likewise, include personality traits you are proud to have, skills you mastered, compliments received, times you were kind or helpful, ideas you were responsible for, people you are delighted to have influenced or affected. The list is pretty much endless.

You'll notice that there's a little overlap between this exercise and the 'Telling the story of your strengths' exercise back in Chapter 4. I'd suggest that you *don't* look back at that exercise to begin with. Some people who look back at the log books of their lives tend to focus on work-related or more tangible achievements. But your FACTs could include anything that *you* define as a Feat, Achievement, Challenge overcome, or Triumph.

Write down all that you've done in your life and you may suddenly think: 'Wow. I have achieved a lot.' And you can continue to achieve more.

Keep adding to your list. Put it aside for a few hours or days and come back to it. Keep it by your bedside and jot any thoughts that come to mind as you're falling asleep or waking up. Your list of FACTs is always a work-in-progress rather than a completed list because you'll keep adding to it. Every time you complete a task or accomplish a goal, you will add it to your list, and help your confidence to bloom and grow.

Once you start to write down a few answers, you'll probably find that you'll open up a floodgate of FACTs that demonstrate the many successes in your life. But if you find yourself stalling, you're not alone. The biggest stumbling block for some people in completing this exercise is that they tend to look only for major successes. They discount too much of what they have achieved. Your own list will be personal to you, but here are some examples from the lists of other people to prompt your thinking:

- 'Completed 14 essay projects and an extended dissertation as part of my studies.'
- 'I've raised two children who have turned into healthy, responsible, happy adults.'
- 'Getting promoted to area manager.'
- 'Moving away from home and becoming financially independent of my parents.'
- 'Keeping the promise I made to Kate on her fortieth birthday and going on six dates in the last year.'
- 'Took my son to football practice and sat there, watching and encouraging and keeping him company, twice a week, for five years!'
- 'Exceeding my performance targets and getting an 'A' rating from my manager the last two years running.'
- 'Setting up the wireless network at home.'
- 'Giving a presentation at the departmental away-day and receiving positive comments on it in spite of how self-conscious I felt.'
- 'Buying my own place, doing it up and turning it into my home and sanctuary.'
- 'I feel good when my daughter spontaneously gives me a hug or tells me she loves me.'
- 'Passing my driving test the first time – despite being so panicky I had a migraine and had to lie down afterwards!'

Over to you

Even if you don't have the time to write out a full list of FACTs, at least get started by jotting down a handful of FACTs right now. Ask yourself:

- What are you pleased to have achieved recently?

- When have you been valued by a person or a group?

- When did you act on your beliefs and do something that was important to you?

- When did you have power or influence over a person, group, or situation?

Enriching your FACT list

Capturing the FACTs of your life is a pretty, er, factual exercise. But to help engage all of your senses when you need to conjure up happier times, consider pulling together mementoes and reminders that trigger positive memories. The idea is to enrich the list of your FACTs so that you have a powerful bank of memories and recollections of when you felt at your happiest and most confident. Your list will differ, but consider assembling collateral such as:

- awards, trophies or certificates – even if these stretch back to your childhood, they can often still provoke strong positive recollections

- letters or congratulatory cards from people

- jewellery, keepsakes, or favourite items of clothing

- items from work such as your first payslip, an old diary chronicling particularly good days or weeks at work, the business cards of people you loved working with, and so on

- souvenirs, books, and even fragrances

- quotations, words, and sounds – including music or poems

■ videos and photos of treasured moments, on holiday, a party at work, getting married, celebrating a birthday, and so on.

Even once you've assembled your basic box, you should continue to collect items and memorabilia that you can put into your confidence bank. Every time you experience a success or feel-good moment, think of how you can capture it. Take a photo, pick up a pebble from a beach, buy a postcard, write a few notes in a diary, or do whatever helps you to aid your future recollection.

Replaying your FACTs

Now we get to what you can do with your FACTs. When you're feeling in the need of a pick-me-up, simply find at least 10 minutes to relive your past triumphs. Replay whichever moments seem most appropriate. Play back the situation and immerse yourself in the sights, sounds, smells, and feelings that went with them. Remember how capable, content, and confident you felt. Avoid analysing them or trying to figure out exactly why they make you happy or what you can learn from them. Just savour the moments as clearly as you can.

Consider assembling a folder of particularly relevant memorabilia and memories to boost your confidence when you're preparing for a particular challenge in your life. For example, if you haven't been socialising much lately, pull together a dossier about the friends you have made over the years. If you're going on a date, gather a folio to remind yourself of your interests and positive traits.

If they can do it ...

Caroline is 52 years old. She has worked for her entire life in publishing and for the last 14 years has been the editor of an airline's in-flight magazine. However, a takeover by a larger competitor and a management reshuffle means that Caroline finds herself out of work. She feels more than a flutter of anxiety about the prospect of having to go for job interviews.

She applied for jobs and got invited to a handful of interviews. Of course she researched the organisations, thought about probable interview questions and how she would respond to them, and rehearsed her answers at home in front of a mirror. But that's the easy bit for her as she knows her industry and job inside and out. What worries her is that she sometimes struggles to project her confidence with new people. So she decides to assemble a confidence file of materials to help her feel and act more confidently.

On the morning of her first interview, she makes breakfast as usual and spends a half-hour flicking through the contents of her confidence file. While other candidates might be going through a last-minute interview drill, she reads about her own successes. Amongst her confidence collateral are copies of the magazines that she has been responsible for, a handwritten letter of encouragement from her best friend, a printout of an email from her ex-boss congratulating her on a particular achievement. She looks at a photo of the team's last Christmas dinner and thinks about all of the people that she has hired and coached over the years. She savours the feelings as she reads the message in a good luck card sent by her 8-year-old nephew.

Not only does the portfolio help to banish her nerves, but she actually feels ready to give the interview her best shot.

Focusing on the here and now

Have you ever found yourself lying in bed at night, your head buzzing with worries and unable to sleep? Well, you're not alone, as surveys show that up to one in three adults may suffer from the occasional bout of insomnia.

When you've got a scary event – a presentation, exam, date – coming up, your head may be filled with anxious thoughts about what you must remember to do or what could go wrong. But I'm sure you know – worrying about it when you should be sleeping isn't terribly productive.

This next Confidence Booster is based on a technique that has been around for a long time. Zen Buddhist monks have been practising the art of mindfulness for thousands of years. All that we modern-day psychologists have done is taken the best of the technique and adapted it so that anyone can use it.

Confidence Booster: Becoming mindful

Mindfulness is essentially about experiencing the present, rather than dwelling on the past or worrying about the future. The basic idea is simple: to keep your attention focused on what you're experiencing right now without allowing your inner voice to comment on it. To become aware of what's going on around you, but without letting your self-talk pass judgement on it.

Most people find that their inner voices constantly chatter about what goes on around them. Hear a police siren go off in a nearby street and you wonder what the emergency is. See a cute puppy and you think 'Oh, how lovely!' Catch a glimpse of your own reflection in the mirror and you think 'I look good' or 'I look bad' depending on your mood. As I sit writing this chapter, I can hear the sound of the boiler pumping water into the radiator in my office, so I'm thinking it must be cold outside. But mindfulness is about stilling *all* of these thoughts – whether they are good, bad, or neutral. It's the ability to empty your mind of thoughts and create an oasis of calm.

You can be mindful whether you are lying in bed trying to get to sleep, sitting at your desk worrying about something you need to do, or walking down the street. You can use mindfulness at any time that you need to empty your head of worrisome thoughts.

- Ensure that your body is relaxed and comfortable. If stress is causing you to tense your shoulders or putting a furrow on your brow, let your muscles go slack. Take a slow, deep breath. Exhale. And close your eyes.

- Focus on the sensation of your own breathing. Avoid changing the way you breathe. Simply notice what it feels like.

- You may notice your inner voice putting thoughts into your head. That's normal. But now you are going to send your voice away from you. You'll still be able to hear it, but you're going to put some distance between you and it, so that it doesn't speak quite so loudly in your head.

- Imagine that each of your thoughts is a car on a road at night. The road is lit by street lamps and stretches into the distance at both ends. But everything else around it is pretty dark. To begin with, you're standing on the pavement by the street. Now, see in your mind's eye the street receding away from you. Imagine that you are flying backwards, away from the street. You can still see the cars driving along the street, but it is far enough away from you that you can't make out any detail about the cars.

- You may spot occasional thoughts popping into your head – that's perfectly OK. But simply allow them to pass by, like cars on that distant street, without engaging with them or trying to suppress them. Aim to maintain this mental state for at least 10 minutes.

With mere minutes of mindfulness, you can let go of all the thoughts rushing around in your head. You can hush the internal chatter. Break a cycle of worrying and shed feelings of anxiety, fear, regret, or anything else. Simply let them pass you by.

You can use mindfulness in all sorts of situations – not just when you are trying to sleep or relax. I coached someone who was letting his worries get the better of him even when he was exercising. He lived in the countryside and went for regular runs after work. But despite passing through beautiful scenery, he was actually mulling over mistakes and recent situations that he had handled badly or worrying about the events of the next day. Even listening to music while he ran made no difference as he admitted blocking out the music with his worrisome thoughts. Training him to become more mindful while he went on his evening runs enabled him to enjoy his exercise and unwind more effectively.

The more you use mindfulness, the better you will get at it and the greater the potential benefits. Dr Sara Lazar at Harvard Medical School in the US found that mindfulness training is associated with a thickening of the insula, the brain area that processes emotion. In the same way that your muscles respond to physical exercise, your brain grows stronger in response to mental exercise. Continued mindfulness may help you to grow a thicker, stronger brain that is more able to deal with emotions. Wow.

Get ready to succeed

Learn to distinguish between productive thought and unproductive worry. Sure, if you need to make a plan or organise an event, you need to spend productive time thinking it through. But worrying when you should be sleeping, dining out with friends, reading, making love – come on, that's not achieving anything. A quick tip to unload your worries is to keep a notepad handy at all times. If you have a specific thought about what you must remember to do running around in your head, pick up a pen and write it down. Once you've got it down on paper, you can rest assured you won't forget to do it. And you can focus on what you should be trying to do.

A few of my coaching clients are a bit sceptical when I suggest mindfulness as a technique for banishing worries. They think they are too smart, fast-paced, idea-filled, or imaginative to benefit from it. But the exact opposite is true: the more you tend to think, the more you need to switch off occasionally. Mindfulness *works*.

Take a crack at it right now. Whether you're reading this in your favourite chair at home or are surrounded by fellow commuters on a busy train, focus your attention on what is going on around you without thinking about it. Put this book down for a moment and turn your mobile phone off. Close your eyes if it helps you to concentrate (and it's safe to do so!). Simply observe the sounds you hear, the sensations you feel, the thoughts that pass through your head. Do it for five minutes and notice how you feel afterwards.

The squishy stuff that surrounds our brains

The squishy stuff that surrounds your brain is of course your body. And while most of this book has focused on stuff that goes on in your mind – your thoughts and feelings – we can't neglect our bodies.

A friend of mine, a management consultant, is totally focused on building a successful business. His business has quadrupled in size in the last few years but he's always complaining about his health. He is constantly busy with his work and he keeps saying that he needs to get fit and lose the extra pounds he has put on lately. He's seeing a physiotherapist at the moment about a niggling shoulder injury. And he seems incredibly prone to coughs and colds – although he calls them 'man flu'. I'm sure that if he could be more confident about his physical health, he could achieve more in his professional life too. I imagine that not being out of breath from climbing a single flight of stairs, not having to worry about his dodgy shoulder, and being able to meet clients without hacking and sneezing, would help him to succeed in his career as well.

"Life is not living, but living in health."

Martial, Roman poet

Your mind and body are not two separate systems. One cannot survive without the other. And no matter how well you train your mind to think more constructively, you will let yourself down if your body isn't similarly well-honed. Even if your confidence goals are completely focused on the work or social or family or sexual spheres of your life, remember that you can't do anything unless the machine that is your physical body is in good shape too.

But I'm not going to lecture you on what to do. Let's face it; you probably already know the kind of things to do. Eat less processed rubbish and munch more fresh fruit and vegetables. Drop the sugary drinks and chug more water. Quit the cigarettes and go easy on the alcohol. Get some regular exercise. You're smart enough to know what you should be doing. You've probably been putting it off and waiting for the 'right' time. Why not make that moment today?

Over to you

What three actions could you take to ensure that your physical body is as nourished as your mind?

▨ I will ....

▨ I will ....

▨ I will ....

Steer clear of the booze and pills

Staying on the topic of feeding your body and mind, let's talk about drugs.

A friend of mine was so petrified of giving the best man's speech at a wedding that he was considering asking a friend who was a doctor to prescribe him a sedative on the sly. I don't know whether he managed to get hold of one in the end. But drugs and alcohol are not long-term solutions; they merely dim your awareness of your surroundings.

Of course there may be situations in which a doctor may prescribe a drug. But always remember that it's not a long-term solution.

There's a saying in psychological circles: 'Feel better, get worse; feel worse, get better.' Sure, having a drink or popping a pill may help you to feel better in the short term. But you don't learn. Your confidence deteriorates. You learn only to become dependent on the drug. The best option may be to feel worse, but get better. Feel worse in the short term, anxious, worried, nauseous even. But by tackling the situation, you get better at it each time. To successfully conquer the situation that you feel anxious about, you need to experience some degree of discomfort for your mind to desensitise and get used to it.

Becoming more confident is not always an easy path. But you are stronger than you may feel. So take positive action and remember that when you behave with confidence, you will come to think confidently and feel confident too.

Your tick-tock resource

Do you spring out of bed in the morning ready to face the world or do you become most awake when the sun goes down? Common wisdom as well as research show that most people can be divided into those who prefer mornings ('larks') or evenings ('owls'). Early birds tend to wake early, prefer to start early in the day, and are at their best during the hours of daylight. Owls prefer afternoons and evenings to mornings, and work well late into the night.

Respect when your body and mind are most awake. Think about the best time of day for you to take on formidable challenges. Whether you need to study for an exam, squeeze in a gym workout, or have a difficult discussion with someone, consider when you're most switched on.

I'm an owl. I enjoy going to the gym in the evenings and shudder at the thought of exercising early in the day. I do my best work at night too – I've on occasion found myself working until 2 or 3 a.m. because I feel most alive at night. But I dread having to set the alarm – ideally I'd get up at around 10 or 11 every morning! On the other hand, a colleague of mine is the total opposite. She rises early even at weekends and loves the tranquil part of the day before anyone else is awake to catch up on work or indulge in her favourite activities. Don't ask her to stay late in the office though.

Your body clock is a resource that you can draw upon if you know yourself well enough. You probably already know which part of the day you are most drawn to. So which are you – a lark or an owl?

ONWARDS AND UPWARDS

■ You are a unique individual and need to decide for yourself what resources work for you and in what circumstances. Once you identify the reinvigorating rituals that pep you up, be sure to incorporate them into your schedule.

■ The fact that you are unique does not mean that you need be isolated. We are a social species and can draw considerable strength from having the right people around us. But consider too that not all of the people you currently spend time with may be equally good for your well-being and confidence.

■ Your memories form the basis for one of the most powerful resources at your disposal. Make a list of your past successes (your FACTs) and keep adding to it to build up a powerful database to remind you that you are stronger than you may sometimes feel.

- You rob yourself of the present if you spend too much time dwelling on the past or worrying about the future. If you do too much of either, make a concerted effort to focus on the here and now using the mindfulness technique.

- Remember that your body and mind are both part of the overall system that is you. A neglected or abused body is hardly going to help your mind to feel at its most confident.

- Plan challenging activities at times of the day that best suit you. Whether you are a lark or an owl, learn to respect when you feel at your best rather than forcing yourself to go against your nature.

Dealing confidently with setbacks

"What is the difference between an obstacle and an opportunity? Our attitude toward it. Every opportunity has a difficulty and every difficulty has an opportunity."
J. Sidlow Baxter, theologian

In this chapter you will ...

- come to appreciate that *everyone* experiences temporary setbacks and that adversity is a necessary part of personal growth
- train yourself to treat setbacks as obstacles to be overcome rather than signs to give up
- discover ways to deal with the emotional fallout of difficult situations
- apply techniques to find novel and effective ways to tackle problems
- learn to look for the positives in every situation.

Everyone experiences setbacks and disappointments. Hardly anyone ever gets what they want on the first attempt. Even the most talented candidates sometimes get rejected from job interviews or overlooked for promotion. Lively, sociable people get turned down for dates. And entrepreneurs often get turned away dozens or even hundreds of times from potential investors and customers. Such knock-backs could dent your self-confidence – but only if you let them.

And then there are the unexpected challenges that life can throw at us such as redundancy, unforeseen relationship troubles, ill-health, the death of a loved one, or other sudden changes in circumstance. Again, such events could make us feel badly about ourselves and want to retreat from the world, but it doesn't have to be that way.

The question isn't whether you'll experience setbacks and difficulties. Everyone does. It's whether you'll recover quickly, grow stronger and learn from them. And in this chapter I tell you how.

From setback to superstar success

Let's look at some famous 'failures'.

James Dyson wanted to create a new type of vacuum cleaner. He made 5,127 attempts before he succeeded in creating a working prototype of the bag-less vacuum cleaner that is now the best-selling vacuum cleaner in the world. Do you think he ever felt down? Of course. But he carried on anyway.

The athlete Dame Kelly Holmes had a running career blighted by numerous injuries – the British press weren't kind and were quick to label her a failure. She felt so low at times she even cut herself with a pair of scissors. But she won two Olympic gold medals in 2004.

Winston Churchill was defeated in every election for public office for most of his career. It wasn't until he was 62 years old that he was finally elected prime minister.

'Queen of Pop' Madonna didn't hit the big time for years. While going for countless auditions, she had to work in a doughnut shop to pay her way. Being rejected time and time again by record producers who told her that she couldn't sing, she could easily have given up. But she didn't.

Nobody gets it right *all* of the time – not even famous entrepreneurs, sports people, entertainers, and world leaders. If you fail to get the result you want, tell yourself that 'you can't win them all' and then figure out what you could do right next time instead.

Confidence Booster: Building your resilience

When we're scared of taking a risk or pursuing an opportunity, most of our concerns are imagined rather than real. Asking someone out on a date or standing up to a bullying colleague may feel scary, but won't actually kill us. One way to develop our hardiness is by taking more small risks every day.

So look for ways to change something in your life every day. Perhaps take a different route to work or try a new breakfast cereal. Sit next to someone different during a meeting at work or go to a different supermarket on the way home. Go for a walk somewhere you've never been on a day off. Get used to saying 'yes' to opportunities too when friends ask you to go somewhere you usually wouldn't go or do something you've not tried. Even if you don't enjoy the experience or it doesn't work out quite as you'd hoped, you will still learn something about yourself that you wouldn't have done if you had simply stuck with what you know.

When we get used to venturing out in small ways, we help to prepare ourselves for the occasions in which we may need to take on bigger leaps such as deciding to move in with a new partner, taking a new job, and so on. So set yourself a daily goal. Think of this as a daily inoculation, a virtual pill to immunise you against bigger knocks in life. What could you do *today*?

"There is no such thing as failure, only feedback."

Robert Allen, writer

You have a choice

Suppose you get passed over for promotion or your proposal for funding gets turned down. Say you go on a date and afterwards your date doesn't return your calls. Or you've been practising for months but you don't make the team for the big game. How would you feel? Would you be tempted to give up?

Confident people experience setbacks, get rejected, dropped, turned down, dumped, and look foolish. But they don't let it get the better of them. When they don't get the result they want, they try again or try something new. They get knocked down again and again, but they get up again and again. They learn from their situations and decide to forge on regardless. They see setbacks, rejection, and adversity as obstacles to be conquered rather than barriers that can't be surmounted.

You can adopt this confident perspective too. Of course you may sometimes *feel* down or *feel* like giving up. But remember: *do, think, feel*. You can choose to *do* something rather than be overcome by how you feel. Choose to *do* something that overrides how you feel; don't let your feelings determine what you do.

"If you are going through hell, keep going."

Winston Churchill, former prime minister

Get ready to succeed

By all means say 'I failed at this task' but never say '*I* am a failure'. Confident people remember that failure does not make *them* failures. You wouldn't call your friends names like 'loser' or 'failure', so resist attaching such labels to yourself. See a setback as a temporary situation rather than a permanent state of being, a detour rather than a dead-end street.

But you may wonder: what if your circumstances are beyond your control? You can't control who your boss gives the promotion to, or whether someone loves you back. And I say: sure, you can't always control what happens to you, but you *can* control how you respond. When faced with a setback, you can use it as an excuse to give up or carry on regardless. Get passed over for promotion and you could feel miserable and give up. Or ask what you need to do differently to get promoted the next time a vacancy comes around. Get dumped and you could mope at home listening to sad songs and refusing to go out. Or chalk it up to experience and get on with the rest of your social life.

What's done is done. Time to leave it behind. There's no point blaming other people or the circumstances for what's happened. So focus instead on what you can change – what *you can do* next.

Over to you

Think about your own life for a moment. List the things you can and cannot control in your own life.

Stuff I *can* control:

- ....

- ....

- ....

Stuff I *can't* control:

- ....

- ....

- ....

Take another look at the list of factors you think you can't control. Are you 100 per cent, totally sure you can't change them, influence them, budge them even a little? If you're certain, make a commitment to ignore them. No point worrying about stuff you can't control. Focus instead on the things you can.

Coping in a crunch

OK, so how can you cope when things go wrong?

Before I answer that question, let me take you on a diversion into evolutionary psychology. Most animals are instinctive creatures – they don't wonder what they fancy for dinner or arrange to meet up with friends at the weekend. Humans are unique in that we can think rationally and make plans. Or at least we can most of the time. Because when we feel threatened, we don't think clearly. We react instinctively, irrationally, emotionally instead.

Ever heard of the fight-or-flight-or-freeze response? All animals – including us humans – have an in-built, pre-programmed response mechanism that's designed to protect us from danger. When our ancestors were faced by ferocious predators, the fight-or-flight-or-freeze system in their brains helped them to respond quickly and effectively. They didn't have the luxury of time to ponder what to do. They'd fight off the predator, flee, or freeze in the hope of not being spotted.

Modern-day problems don't usually run the risk of being eaten alive. Yet we still revert to our pre-programmed fight-or-flight-or-freeze response. In a crunch, you may start to get angry even if there is no one to fight. You may experience panic and want to flee the situation. Or you may freeze with indecision.

Luckily, you can short-circuit the fight-or-flight-or-freeze response and put yourself back in control. You can respond in a more appropriate and effective way simply by asking yourself a handful of questions.

Confidence Booster: Taking the STRAIN out

STRAIN stands for six questions to work through when you're feeling stressed. Whether a burst pipe is flooding your home or a colleague has humiliated you in public, you've made a social gaffe about the bride at her wedding, or you've just been fired, these questions allow you to take a time out. You can defuse the emotion from a setback or situation and choose to respond in a rational, effective fashion.

- ■ **Scale**. *How big a deal is this on a scale of 0 to 10?* When we're stressed, we often blow things out of proportion, thinking that it's the worst thing that could possibly happen. But is anyone's life in danger?

Is anyone going to repossess your home or take your children away? Those are 9s and 10s. So how much of an impact is this current crisis going to score?

■ **Time**. *How much of an issue will this be in six months' time?* With the benefit of hindsight, we know that what seemed awful yesterday often turns out to be not so bad today. And what was terrible last month may be but a passing memory or even a funny story to share. So when you're in the middle of a situation, consider how it might look with the passing of time. Is it really so awful that it's still going to be causing you grief in six months' time?

■ **Response**. *Has your response so far been appropriate and effective?* Perhaps you've buried your head in the sand and hoped the problem would go away. Maybe you felt furious, or tearful, or decided to give up. Asking yourself about the suitability and value of whatever you've done so far will ensure you don't continue to behave unproductively.

■ **Action**. *What actions could you take now to improve the situation?* What's done is done. Whatever happened has already happened; it's in the past. If something failed or something got broken or someone let you down, it can't be changed. All you can do now is decide on what to do in the present. So whether your response so far has been mildly constructive or dramatically unsuccessful, you need to look at how you could move forward. Decide on the emotions you wish to feel as well as the actions you want to take. Sometimes failure signals that it's time for a different tactic. If what you've done so far hasn't worked, then doing almost anything else will probably be better. So what will you do?

■ **Implications**. *What would you do differently next time?* Once the dust has settled – whether that's hours or weeks later – ask yourself how you could avoid getting into the same situation and repeating the same mistake. How would you deal with a similar situation or ideally prevent it from happening at all?

■ **Nourishing thought**. *What can you find that is positive in the situation?* There's a saying that when one door closes, another opens. By looking for the positive in your situation, you learn to take a positive, constructive, nourishing perspective on the situations you find yourself in.

The 'N' in STRAIN reminds us to look for a nourishing thought, because what initially seems a setback can lead to learnings or even create opportunities elsewhere.

I got fired from a job once. They told me that I was rubbish at the work and that I should pack my bags. I wasn't happy – downright miserable in fact. But another job came along that paid more and suited my skills better – my new boss encouraged me to pursue my interests, which meant writing books like this one. To cut a long story short, one of my books caught the attention of the BBC, who gave me my own TV series – presenting a show helping people to get their dream jobs. An experience that remains one of my career highlights. But I would never have had it if I hadn't been fired.

Some of life's most valuable lessons and opportunities really are disguised as setbacks at the time. Sometimes *very* cleverly disguised! It may only be with a bit of time and perspective that you can recognise them as the lessons or nourishing situations they are.

If they can do it ...

A friend of mine got dumped a couple of years ago. Let's call her Cheryl. She had a young daughter and thought she was happily married, but her husband fell for someone at work and walked out. The divorce forced Cheryl to move into a smaller house, look for a new job, and cope as a single parent. Fast forward to the present though and she's a director of a successful business and she has a new love in her life – a handsome skiing instructor!

Over to you

Perhaps you don't believe me that setbacks can often be opportunities. Believe yourself instead. Take five minutes to jot down answers to the following questions:

- What, on the surface of it, was the best 'mistake' or apparent setback of *your* life?

- What happened?

- Why did you consider it a mistake or setback?

- What lessons did you learn? How have those lessons helped you since?

- What opportunities came out of the situation?

- What does the event tell you about the nature of success versus 'failure'?

Forward not back

It's an all-too-human trait to give ourselves grief over what we *should* have done. But it's easy to give ourselves a hard time with the benefit of hindsight. Of course we *now* realise that we should have been more assertive, said yes to that party invitation, asked that attractive guy or gal out. That we shouldn't have blurted out our opinion, parked the car on the double yellow lines, or embarked on that disastrous relationship. But it happened, and that's fine. Time to move on.

The STRAIN questions help you to look forward, not back. OK, your response so far may not have worked out. But what action can you take to move forward? How would you handle or avoid the situation next time? What is the positive, the lesson learned, the new opportunity that has been created?

There's nothing mystical in these six questions, but they work. By going through the discipline of asking yourself these questions, you reboot your brain. Like hitting the reset button, you eliminate the emotional turmoil and allow your rational, problem-solving mind to take over.

I know clients who scribble the questions on the inside of their notepads or simply write the word STRAIN on a sticky note to keep in prominent and permanent view. Discipline yourself to do it and you will take confident action even in the worst of times.

Making confident choices, choices, choices

The STRAIN questions are a powerful tool for cutting through emotion and pushing through to find a useful solution. However, the course of action to take is not always clear. You may have several choices with distinct advantages and disadvantages to each. Take the new job and you'll have more responsibility and a large bonus but have to spend longer commuting each way to work. Choose to end an unsatisfactory relationship but risk not meeting anyone more suitable. Decide to report a colleague who is bullying someone else in the team but risk being dragged into a lengthy legal process.

> "Take risks: if you win, you will be happy; if you lose, you will be wise."
>
> **Anonymous**

When a clear choice does not spring up at you, you may benefit from taking a systematic approach to weighing up your choices and deciding what to do. Writing a letter to yourself is a powerful technique for loosening knotty situations. Go ahead, use it – you may be surprised at how effective the result can be.

Confidence Booster: Corresponding with your inner coach

Imagine that you are your own best friend. Write yourself a letter as if you are summarising a friend's situation, the choices they are faced with, and the solution they should take. Start the letter 'Dear {your name}' and start writing. Work through the following steps:

1 **Outline your problem or dilemma**. Take a clean sheet of paper and write about the situation. Even if you don't know what to write, just start writing. Perhaps start with the phrase 'The situation as I see it is that you …' Once you see your first few sentences written down, you may find that other words seem to flow from them. Make sure you describe both what's happening and how you feel about it.

2 **Generate possible options**. Write down all of the alternatives for dealing with the situation. Even if you are faced with what seems initially to be a black-or-white, all-or-nothing decision, you may find that there are subtle variations on each option. For example, rather than deciding to stay with your partner or leave forever, you could have a temporary separation or stay but pursue couples counselling. A temporary separation could be for a few weeks if you moved in with a friend or six months if you rented your own place. With a little thought, you may uncover more options than you first thought.

3 **Weigh up pros and cons**. Write down what you see as the advantages and disadvantages of each option. But think in particular about how each option would make you *feel*. By writing down pros and cons, you can more easily see how certain courses of action might be more constructive than others.

4 **Choose a small, positive step to take**. By moving away from an all-or-nothing view of your situation, you may be able to identify a small step you can take in the right direction of one of your options.

A common trap for many people is to get stuck worrying about the 'right' option to take. But if you toy with options continually without making a decision, you can't move forward. You suffer paralysis by analysis. By not choosing, you *are* choosing – to remain helpless.

But take action and you make progress. If you choose to do something that you don't enjoy, you at least learn what you don't like; if you make a mistake, you at least discover what doesn't work. Taking an action often informs what your next step should be. Doing *something* is almost always better than doing nothing.

Throughout your letter, include a description not only of what's going on but also of how you feel. Include your emotions as well as the facts. Do it because research shows that including your feelings can help you to find more effective solutions. For example, one group of researchers looked at people who had been made redundant. People who wrote about the thoughts and feelings they had about losing their jobs found new jobs more quickly than those who didn't. It isn't just an airy-fairy technique for releasing emotions – it provides practical solutions. So write about feelings as well as facts because it will make you more successful.

I coach someone who types an email and actually sends it to himself so that the email sits in his inbox, summarising his situation and his solution. A woman I coach bought a pack of expensive writing paper to compose her letter to herself. Then again, the technique is just as effective if you scribble your notes on a sheet of cheap paper or into your journal too.

If they can do it ...

At the age of 36, Gemma has a 14-month-old son and is struggling to decide whether to go back to work or not. She enjoyed her work as a corporate lawyer. But at the same time she doesn't want to return to work and end up regretting not seeing her son grow up. Feeling more than a little uncertain, this is the letter she writes to herself.

Dear Gemma,

By the end of the year, Jonathan will be 2 years old. But now you're wondering if you should go back to work or not.

You do miss the buzz of work. You miss having clients ask you for advice and having colleagues to chat to. The money is great and you like being noticed as a successful, professional woman too. There's also the intellectual challenge of finding ways to sort out clients' problems – you don't get the same kind of mental workout in looking after Jonathan.

Looking after Jonathan is a completely different sort of challenge. Of course you love him and are glad to have him. But he tests your patience rather than your intellect. Yes, I think you realise that you need some sort of intellectual stimulation. But what should that stimulation be?

By going back to work, you worry about missing out on his early years. And perhaps part of the reason you don't want to go back to work is because your own mother took a break from her career and never went back. You had a great childhood. Your mother was always there for you. But is that what you want for your own life?

OK, so let's think of other options. I guess you could quit law and do something else entirely. You like photography and you've become a real expert taking beautiful photos of Jonathan recently – is there a way you could turn your hobby into a career? Then there's retraining in a different field. That would be intellectually exciting but expensive and probably as demanding as going back to the law firm full time – although maybe you shouldn't rule it out for now.

You could work part time. Although that would be difficult working for Briggs & Smith as they work with such large international clients who always have such pressing deadlines. So maybe you could leave the firm and join a client organisation where you'd be under less pressure and be able to work maybe four days a week. Another option would be to find a smaller law firm that specialises in smaller projects.

Yet another alternative would be to look after Jonathan for a few more years – say until he goes off to school in two years' time. You could always find some kind of reading or project to keep your brain ticking over. Or you could get a part-time job doing something unrelated to the law for a few years until he goes to school.

Weighing up those options, I can tell that you don't really want to go back to your old job. The work was so demanding. Imagine how little you'd get to see Jonathan! But you do want to go back to work. You love Jonathan but you don't want to invest all of your energy bringing him up only to have nothing left of yourself once he is grown up. So you do need to work.

You trained as a lawyer and you love being an expert in your field, so it's either law or another profession that uses your brain. Photography is a nice idea but it's not demanding in the way you want – you're not going to get the same mental buzz. And it's probably not going to earn enough money to live on either.

So it sounds like you need to find a job with a smaller law firm where the clients won't be quite so demanding and you can work maybe four days. If you don't like it after three months, you can always try to get your old job back. They've kept it open for you for two years so another three months isn't going to hurt, is it?

Yes, I would recommend that you get on to the internet and start looking for jobs in smaller law firms.

Yours,
(Your inner coach) Gemma

So when can you test-drive this technique? Make a decision to use it soon. OK, you may not have the time to try it right now. But at least make a commitment to set aside a mere 15 minutes of your time – that's only 1 per cent of one day! – in the coming weeks to give it a go. Think about a quandary or situation that is troubling you. Maybe you're not certain whether to take one of a number of options or you're struggling even to see what your options might be. Use the technique and see what you come up with.

Handling the weight of the world

No one is immune from the experiences of loss and disappointment. You can't cut yourself off from your emotions. Negative emotions such as sadness, fear, and anger have crucial roles to play in our lives. Imagine not being able to experience grief over the loss of a loved one, fear in the presence of genuine danger, or anger when you have been treated unfairly. These emotions are an important part of what make us human. They alert us that something is wrong and needs to be put right. To be rid of such feelings would make you a robot – or a vegetable.

Sometimes you may need to feel the full weight of your emotions. Pull your blinds down or close your curtains and have a good cry. Weep and wail and let the tears come tumbling down. Or shut yourself away from the world to scream and shout to express how you really feel. It can be healthy to let it all out – for a while.

Having said that, you can manage your emotions more effectively, no matter how badly you may feel. Because people can and do cope with all sorts of terrible circumstances. Many people who experience tragedies such as life-threatening illness or losing a loved one manage to continue with their lives. They soldier on rather than wallowing in their feelings for too long. They feel as sad, hurt, and distraught as the other people who give up on themselves and their lives. The only difference is that they choose to carry on regardless.

In spite of how they feel, they take action. They make plans, they set goals in life, they get out and carry on with their work and friends and lives. *Do, think, feel.* By taking action, they gradually think differently and feel differently too. By choosing to behave as if they feel confident, they enable themselves to think confidently and feel confidently as well.

If they can do it ...

Leanne is a 27-year-old friend of mine. Some years ago, she had pain in her foot and went to hospital. They told her she had cancer: a tumour in her left foot. After a year of painful radiotherapy and operations, she had to have her left leg amputated. She was only 20 at the time.

She would have had every right to feel sorry for herself. To cry and complain about the unfairness of the world and ask for others to take pity on her. But she didn't.

In fact she decided to organise a charity auction to raise money for Macmillan Cancer Support. She convinced millionaires to lend her the use of their private jets. She persuaded local businesses to give her prizes for her auction. She invited hundreds of guests to bid on the prizes. And she raised over £100,000 for charity on a single day.

But it doesn't stop there. She went on to put together a fitness video for people with disabilities. And the last time I spoke to her, she had just signed a book deal to write an autobiography, the uplifting story of how a young woman has triumphed in the face of adversity.

You can't always control what happens to you, but you can control how you respond.

The STRAIN questions are a great way of coping with adversity. And writing yourself a letter is useful if you're stuck for a solution. But sometimes you're not looking for an answer. Just a way to feel better.

You'd like to move on since you got dumped, had that illness, got fired. Or you're already trying to get on with your life. But you still feel too upset, angry, afraid, ashamed, guilty, whatever. The emotions are too strong, they feel overwhelming. If that's the case, you can use this next technique to accelerate your emotional recovery. Rather than be the casualty of your emotions, you can help yourself to feel better. Even if you can't bring yourself to get back out into the real world, you can at least put pen to paper.

Confidence Booster: Expressing negative emotions away

Expressive writing is a potent tool for easing the burden of negative emotions. You aren't looking for an answer – you just want to feel better as quickly as you can. To get the most out of it, you will need to repeat this technique for 30 minutes for between three and five consecutive days.

Choose a time and place in which you can concentrate for half an hour, free from distractions. Then spend the first 15 to 20 minutes writing (or typing) about how you *feel*. This isn't about finding a solution – just capturing your feelings. You must include in your writing two topics:

- the difficult experience or emotional issue that is affecting you
- your vision and goals in life moving forward (and here it may help you to think back to your vision and goals from Chapter 4).

Really let go and explore your deepest emotions and thoughts. You are writing this for no one but yourself, so be totally honest no matter what you may be thinking and feeling. Don't worry about spelling, grammar, or sentence structure. The only rule is that once you begin writing, you continue for at least 15 minutes (or longer if you wish).

Rather than write into the journal you usually use, take separate sheets of paper or a fresh document on your computer. Once you have finished writing, you may wish to seal them away in a box or envelope, symbolically distancing yourself from the difficult experience and the emotions that go with it.

However, here's a health warning: you may actually feel worse immediately after writing about your feelings. Research shows that the benefits of expressive writing can take a couple of days to kick in. So an important final step is to spend your last 10 minutes running through the 'three good things' technique (see 'Confidence Booster: Developing your sense of optimism' on page 45). Turn your attention to whatever you feel grateful for in order to pick up your mood again. And remember that you need to repeat this technique for three to five days to get the most from it.

Research shows that expressive writing has helped people to cope more quickly and effectively with all manner of testing situations including divorce, sexual abuse, and job loss. Studies have even shown that people who capture their most traumatic experiences in writing also make fewer visits to the doctor *and* have lower blood pressure. In other words, expressive writing seems to improve not only psychological well-being but physical health too.

No matter how badly you may feel, you have a choice. You can let your circumstances get the better of you. Or you can forge on, take action, at least capture your thoughts on paper, *do* something. Which will you choose?

ONWARDS AND UPWARDS

- Setbacks are inevitable stepping stones on the way to eventual success. Confident people get knocked down but keep, keep, keep getting back up again.

- To experience negative emotions is an essential part of being human. The fight-or-flight-or-freeze response has a vital protective function in keeping you alive.

- We all react emotionally rather than rationally when we feel in a pinch. However, you can make better decisions about how to respond by slowing things down. Use the STRAIN questions to take a deliberate time out.

- Write about your situations and emotions if you want to find solutions or feel better. Something happens between getting your thoughts out of your head and on to paper – it really can help.

- Remember that you always have a choice. Even if you can't control your circumstances, you can choose how you respond. The best way to cope with a setback and escape the funk of dejection is to do something. Don't wait until you feel better to take action. Take action to feel better.

■ And it's so important that I'll say it again: the sooner you take action to change your circumstances, the sooner you will feel better about yourself.

Creating a confident future

"If you don't know where you're going, you will probably end up somewhere else."

Laurence J. Peter, educator

CONFIDENCE

In this chapter you will ...

■ discover a way to feel positive and confident every day

■ review your progress to make sure you are moving in the right direction

■ appreciate that it is both normal and expected to make great progress on some days but stall or even slide backwards on other days

■ take the credit for your successes and make a deliberate effort to celebrate them to keep your motivation high

■ review the exercises we have covered and choose the techniques that work best for you.

We're nearly there. The finish line is in sight and you're almost fully equipped to tackle whatever challenges you want to take on. A handful more tiny techniques to add to your toolkit and you're good to go.

In this final chapter of Part 1 you'll see how to check that you're making progress towards your goals and why celebrating your success is a vital part of realising your confident future.

Growing your confidence every day

By now you should have a vision of the life you'd like to lead and the goals you would like to achieve. But sometimes you may get too busy and may not feel able to make time for working towards your vision and goals. However, you can still help yourself to feel more in control and confident every single day, by starting your mornings by thinking about the mindset you're going to adopt for the day. The beauty of this next Confidence Booster is that it takes less than a minute.

Confidence Booster: Planning your positivity policy

Early on in your day, think back to the vision of the life you'd like to lead and the goals you'd like to achieve. Then decide on an attitude or mindset consistent with your vision and goals that you will adopt for the day to help you feel more positive and confident.

Consider the following examples:

- 'I will approach situations today with a calm mindset.'

- 'I will greet everyone with a smile.'

- 'I will listen before I speak.'

- 'I will allow myself small indulgences.'

- 'I will point out what's good about other people's ideas before saying anything else.'

- 'I will be brave and say yes to an opportunity today.'

This isn't just wishful thinking. This is a small but positive step towards maintaining your sense of optimism, a subtle encouragement to look at opportunities and situations in a better way. Rather than possibly lapsing into negative thinking or bad habits, we make a conscious decision to approach the world in a positive and confident manner.

Making course corrections

Building your confident new future is not a one-time event. On your journey to greater confidence, you need to keep track of how you're doing. If your actions are moving you closer to your goals, you can congratulate yourself and speed ahead. If you hit confidence traffic jams or psychological road blocks, you can investigate alternative routes to get you back on course.

A great way of keeping track is to write up your progress in a diary or journal. You don't have to write much. Perhaps just a couple of bullet points every day or two. Or a few paragraphs every week. But by charting your growth, you can look back and see where you used to be and how you used to feel. You can see how far you've come and keep your motivation high.

Sports coaches, business consultants, and life coaches use a variety of tools to help people measure the ground they've covered and stay on track. I like the GROAN model as a way of checking whether you're doing OK or need to make a course correction.

Confidence Booster: GROANing your way to confidence

The GROAN model is one that I've developed and used to great effect with people ranging from individuals who want to lose weight to managing directors who want to grow their businesses. There are five steps:

- **Goals** – Begin by reminding yourself of your goals. Imagine for a few moments that you have already achieved your goals to jog your memory as to why they are worthwhile.

- **Results** – Ask yourself how much progress you have made. Be honest about it. No point deluding yourself if you're only 50 or 30 or 2 per cent of the way to reaching your goals.

- **Options** – Consider your options for closing the gap between your results and your goals. Even if the results you've achieved so far are in the right direction, ask yourself whether more of the same is what you need. Should you continue as you are, tweak what you're doing, or devise an entirely new approach altogether?

- **Anticipation** – Look ahead to the immediate future. To ensure your continued progress: what possible obstacles or events could crop up to challenge your confidence? And how could you sidestep them?

- **Next steps** – Make sure you decide what you're going to do next. What are the precise steps you will be taking in the next few days or weeks? And when will you do them? Delaying is not a strategy. And neither is hoping that the situation will sort itself out. Make a commitment to take action and stick to it.

"Life is a series of outcomes. Sometimes the outcome is what you want. Great. Figure out what you did right. Sometimes the outcome is what you don't want. Great. Figure out what you did so you don't do it again."

Simone Caruthers, psychologist

Decide for yourself how often you should measure your progress. If you can meaningfully measure how you're doing from one day to the next, by all means work through the GROAN model daily. Keeping a tally of the number of job applications you make every day could be a good idea if your number one priority is to get a new job. If your goal is more long-term, you may wish to review your progress weekly or every couple of weeks. Checking the scales to see how much weight you've lost on a daily basis would be pointless as you'd expect to get fitter over the course of weeks, not days. But you're a sensible person. Work out for yourself how often to review is enough – but not too much.

If they can do it ...

Neela is 23 and for as long as she can remember has found it difficult striking up conversations with new people. She has on more than one occasion been told by people at work and friends of friends that she comes across as disinterested or aloof. She had set herself a goal to grow her circle of friends and has managed to make a few good friends at work. But right now she is struggling to make friends outside of work. She works through the GROAN model to figure out what to do next.

- **Goal**. My goal is to create a group of friends – both from work and away from it – that I can take pleasure spending time with and depend on occasionally. To feel happy and positive about my social life would feel perfect.

■ **Results**. I've made progress with friends at work, but I haven't made a single new friend outside of work. I've invited people over for dinners, but haven't received any invites back. I don't tend to get invited to parties, and when I did go to that one party, I spoke only to the people I already knew. But I know I'm not the kind of person who shines in a group, so maybe dinners and parties aren't right for me.

■ **Options**. I should ask my friends what they think. I've told Anthony and Patricia about how I'd love to have more friends so maybe they'll have some ideas. I could always just get better at talking to random people on the street – I know Beth does that all the time. But I think that's too far outside of my comfort zone right now. I could also join a club or society of some kind.

■ **Anticipation**. I suppose my biggest obstacle is just me. I know what I need to do. It's not that anyone else is stopping me from doing it.

■ **Next steps**. I'll talk to Anthony tomorrow and Patricia when she gets back from holiday next week to see what suggestions they have. And this weekend I'll look on the internet to see what dance or other evening classes I can find in the area that I could join.

Good days and bad

You sometimes hear people say 'I'm only human'. They may shrug and have a mischievous twinkle in their eye because they've been a bit naughty – but they have a point. We aren't robots. We have slips and lapses, make mistakes, give into the occasional temptation. We make progress one day and falter the next. We have good days and bad.

Some people who are trying to build their confidence expect quick and easy results. But that's not how it happens. You may have days when you make no progress or even seem to be taking steps backwards.

If you're on a journey towards the destination of your vision and goals, you will experience obstacles. Some days you may hit a road block or take a wrong turn that may mean a detour before you can carry on again. Or your progress may slow like you're in a bottleneck, so much so that you barely feel you're moving at all. But that's normal and expected. The important thing is to persevere, keep going. You just need to think of your growth in terms of your overall trajectory rather than from one day to the next.

In my teenage years, I used to be a competitive ice figure skater, training four or five times a week. Having mastered the single jumps, I was trying to learn more complex jumps such as the double Salchow and double Axel. I sometimes had a great training session, landing a lot of solid jumps. But the next day, I could end up falling many times. My knees got sore and my butt got wet from sliding around on the melting ice. Of course it was frustrating to compare my progress from one day to the next. But looking at my progress from one season to the next, I got better and better.

A client of mine is building an advertising business. One month she wins four or five new accounts. Occasionally she wins none. But to see how she's doing now against how she was doing a year ago, there's no comparison. She's a mogul in the making – she just needs reminding of it occasionally.

And all of us did it when we were kids. Babies try to walk and end up stumbling for weeks or months before they finally manage to get up on both feet. We don't criticise them for not getting it in one go. So go easy on yourself when you fall down occasionally too.

By all means aspire to be great in the long-term, but allow yourself to be good or even OK in the short-term. You may want to be a superb public speaker, able to wow audiences of thousands with your manner and wit. Great, but that won't come overnight. In the meantime avoid condemning yourself over the little imperfections in the speeches you give. Respect that you continue to make the effort to improve rather than do nothing.

You are trying to be the best that you can, given your current state of mind and personal resources. So give yourself a break. Be your own best friend. Support your efforts and congratulate yourself for what you manage to do rather than put yourself down for what you haven't quite managed. Because at some point you will suddenly look back and realise how far you've come.

Get ready to succeed

Return to the quizzes in Chapter 1 after a period of, say, three or six months. If you diligently apply the Confidence Boosters in this book and complete the exercises – *writing them down*, not doing them in your head – you are certain to see a marked improvement in your confidence.

Celebrating success

Achieving your goals can be habit-forming. Once you start to see your progress, you'll be wanting, actually wanting, more too.

Welcome to the ride that is the circle of confidence. The more you achieve, the more your confidence grows. The more your confidence grows, the more you'll want to achieve. Get a taste of success and you could find yourself craving more, working harder to get it, and achieving more.

However, scientists tell us that the circle of confidence can need our help. Research by scientists using brain-imaging scanners shows that the parts of the brain that are responsible for generating feelings of excitement become activated only when imagining or experiencing short-term rewards rather than distant ones. If your goal is too far in the future, you can't get truly excited about it. You need to celebrate the mini-milestones along the way rather than wait for the big pay-off in however many months' or years' time.

To keep yourself going, you must allow yourself to take credit for your successes. Acknowledge the work you put into achieving your goals. Because only by consciously recognising your talents, skills, and efforts can you achieve the greatest boost to your confidence.

This step isn't optional. In fact, Professor Martin Seligman and his squad of psychologists at the University of Pennsylvania have shown that if you *don't* actively and consciously take responsibility for your achievements, your confidence may actually dwindle. Without paying attention to your achievements and congratulating yourself for your successes, your mind may start to slip into bad thinking habits. You could start to believe that your achievements were down to dumb luck rather than your own efforts.

Contrast a positive versus negative way of thinking about the achievements you realise:

Positive versus negative views on success

Positive views	Negative views
'I deserved to get the job offer because of the research and rehearsal I did.'	'None of the other candidates could have been much good.'
'I built a great rapport with the client and won her over.'	'My colleagues did all the really hard work in making the pitch to the client.'
'I did a good job.'	'I could have done better.'
'I earned that promotion.'	'I got lucky.'
'I put hours into revising for that exam and it paid off.'	'The examiner must have been in a good mood.'

Our old friend the *do, think, feel* loop kicks in even when you aren't consciously aware of it. Say to yourself that your achievement wasn't a big deal or tell a friend that it was nothing and you will *believe* it too. Make a self-deprecating comment in a jokey fashion because you don't want to appear arrogant and you undermine your confidence. Sure, it may take a while, but it will erode your self-assurance in the end. So don't do it!

Find ways of recognising and celebrating your achievements that work for you. Whether it's a major goal that has taken you many months to complete or a smaller goal that you set yourself that very morning, give yourself credit for what you have achieved. If you put in the good day of studying that you set out to do, take that tub of ice cream from the freezer or that ice cold beer from the fridge and savour your success. Survive giving a presentation at your team away-day and you may want to buy yourself a chocolate bar or pint, handbag or pair of designer jeans. Successes vary in size and importance but by considering affordable and appropriate luxuries, you can ensure you stay believing and feeling confident.

Over to you

Have a think now. What small incentives could you use to reward yourself at the end of each successful day? Jot down at least three gifts or activities you could use to celebrate a daily success.

- ....
- ....
- ....

Confidence Booster: Putting the icing on the confidence cake

Celebrating success is not always about spending money. It's as much about acknowledging your successes to yourself. Some people find it easier to congratulate themselves than others do. If you struggle, try one (or both) of these quick techniques to give yourself the credit you are due for your own accomplishments.

■ Write down how you feel about your achievement. Perhaps write about it last thing at night to summarise the successes you had that day – that can be a good way to set yourself up for a good night's sleep. If you're keeping a log of your FACTs (from Chapter 5), make sure you add it there too.

■ Stand in front of a mirror, look your reflection in the eyes, and tell yourself about your achievement out loud. And say it as if you mean it. Imagine that you are celebrating with your best friend and applauding his or her success. If a friend of yours was pleased with an achievement, you wouldn't just say 'That was OK' and change the topic. You would show your excitement and heap praise and compliments on your friend. Let yourself go over the top a bit in sharing the story of your success with yourself.

A final (gentle) kick in the behind

Building a brilliantly confident you isn't rocket science. Sure, there's a lot of science and research behind the tools in this book. Psychologists the world over have put tens of thousands of people through the exercises and techniques in this book, but the tools are not difficult to understand.

I've said it before and I shall say it one last time. The challenge in creating a confident future isn't in understanding what's in this book – it's in *using it*. Nothing can stop your unbridled progress so long as you *do* the exercises and *use* the techniques. Reading about them, nodding sagely and thinking you get the idea isn't good enough. Research by the scientists I've mentioned as well as others tells us in no uncertain terms that people who skip the writing part and decide only to 'think through' the exercises and techniques cheat themselves and get far smaller benefits. You get out of this book what you put into it. Positive thinking by itself isn't enough. Results are achieved by *actions*, not intentions.

"Two little words that can make all the difference – START NOW."

Mary C. Crowley, entrepreneur

The one-off Take Action exercises in this book provide a powerful foundation for your more confident life. Tick off each one as you complete it and you can be sure you are taking huge strides towards the confident new you.

Take Action exercises	✓
1 Doing a CAT scan (pages 34–5)	
2 Learning from the best (page 58)	
3 Dressing for success (pages 62–3)	
4 Telling the story of your strengths (pages 78–9)	
5 Creating your vision (page 80)	
6 Uncovering your values (page 87)	
7 What do you really, really want? (page 97)	
8 Tapping your reserves of confidence (page 114)	
9 Choosing your comrades with care (pages 118–20)	
10 Considering the FACTs of life (pages 122–3)	

I sometimes got emails from readers of the first edition of this book saying that the book didn't work for them. When I asked them how they had found the Take Action exercises, they often replied 'I haven't got round to them yet'! Remember that simply *reading* about the exercises won't help you to become more confident. You have to *do* them!

If the 10 Take Action exercises in this book provide the bedrock, then the 18 Confidence Boosters help you to build a towering pillar of confidence. But as you are a unique individual, what works for you will vary from one situation to the next. For example, what other people find funny may leave you cold. Just because *many* people find a certain film or TV show or comedian hilarious doesn't mean that you will end up laughing out loud too. That doesn't mean that it's not funny – just not funny *for you*. And the same goes for the Confidence Boosters. Use each one a handful of times and see which ones work best for you. You may find that some of them are startlingly powerful while others just don't click for you.

You may find a few of the techniques particularly effective in your personal life while others work best in your work life. You may find some useful when you're in the midst of a challenge and others more suited to preparing for it or dealing with its aftermath. You may feel more comfortable using certain ones when you're alone and others when you're surrounded by people, say at a party or in an open plan office. Or you may be a person who finds it easier to work with words than mental imagery – or vice versa. As you use the Confidence Boosters, make a note of when they hit the right spot for you.

Confidence Booster	When does it work for you?
Creating your cool CATs	
Giving form to your thoughts	
Pondering possibilities	
Developing your sense of optimism	
Using the movie screen in your head	
Diaphragmatic breathing	
Calming your emotions with ABCD	
Muscling out stress	
Performing vocal gymnastics	

Confidence Booster	When does it work for you?
Rut-busting	
Becoming mindful	
Building your resilience	
Taking the STRAIN out	
Corresponding with your inner coach	
Expressing negative emotions away	
Planning your positivity policy	
GROANing your way to confidence	
Putting the icing on the confidence cake	

With these Confidence Boosters, you can take on just about anything that life might throw at you. So the next time you're presented with an opportunity to do something new and different, why not give it a go? You have little to lose – and possibly everything to gain.

So that's it. We're done. Congratulations.

You now have all of the resources you need to craft a more confident life. If you take action daily, your new sense of confidence is assured. Don't wait to feel more confident first – take action to feel more confident. Don't wait for your circumstances to improve or luck to change. Change your circumstances. Make your own luck. Decide what you want and make it happen for you.

ONWARDS AND UPWARDS

- Use the GROAN technique occasionally to check that what you're doing is actually delivering the right results.

- Be kind to yourself and avoid beating yourself up when it comes to reviewing your progress. You wouldn't criticise close friends for all their mistakes, so don't give yourself a hard time when it comes to the little lapses you are bound to make.

- Accept that progress may feel irregular from one day to the next. But so long as you keep moving forward, you will one day suddenly amaze yourself with how far you've come.

- Make a conscious effort to recognise and celebrate your achievements. Without that positive feedback, you may take for granted what you have achieved and undermine your newfound confidence.

- Tick off the exercises and techniques as you use them. But remember: reading about and understanding a technique or exercise is not the same as using it!

Part 2

Confidence when you need it

08

Confident public speaking and presentations

Surveys show that more people are scared of having to speak in public than are scared of snakes, spiders, and getting on a plane put together! And I used to be one of them too.

I used to be so worried about speaking in public that I felt physically sick. My stomach churned and I thought I was going to throw up. But I trained myself to get over the nerves. I now give rather good presentations (and get invited to do so by organisations ranging from colleges and universities to big corporates) and get an enormous buzz out of it as well.

One of the biggest reasons why people lack confidence when speaking is because they haven't done enough preparation – but you have to know the *right* sort of preparation to do. Because a big part of being confident on the big day comes from knowing that everything that *should* go right *will* go right.

Perhaps you need to deliver a speech as the best man or matron of honour. Maybe you need to deliver a project update to your colleagues. Or you need to win over a new client with a clever presentation. Whatever the speech you're giving, work through these 10 steps to boost your confidence and help yourself shine.

1 Find out exactly what you need to do

Your preparation starts by finding out exactly what you are being asked to do.

- **Who will the audience be?** If someone asks you to give a short presentation to 'the senior managers', are they talking about the handful of senior managers within your department or the 237 senior managers from all over Europe? Be careful not to make any assumptions about your audience. The more you know about them, the better you can prepare.
- **How long are you being asked to speak for?** Don't let anyone wave you aside with vague instructions such as 'Oh, just say a

few words, whatever you like.' Get a firm steer on when you should shut up.

■ **What is your audience looking to hear?** Consider what the audience is looking for. Guests at a wedding don't want to listen to long-winded speeches all night. They'd probably appreciate a shorter speech so they can get back to the celebrations! If speaking on a work topic, figure out exactly what the audience is coming to hear – are they looking for information or inspiration or a combination of the two?

■ **What should the tone of your speech be?** Say you're speaking at a birthday party. Can you be risqué for close friends or strictly PG-rated for the sake of the elderly grandmother or younger nephews and nieces? Speaking to clients, should your tone be professional and formal or friendly and informal?

■ **Where will you be speaking?** It makes a difference. If you're speaking in a marquee pitched in someone's back garden, consider whether you'll have a microphone or will have to rely on the strength of your voice to make yourself heard to 200 guests. If you're speaking at a conference, will you have access to a computer and projector or simply be expected to keep the audience's attention with nothing more than a microphone?

Never be afraid to ask lots of questions. Better to get clear guidance on what you need to deliver than be too afraid to ask and end up giving a speech that misses the mark.

2 Engage the passion of your personal perspective

OK, what are you going to say? Start jotting your thoughts down. Have a one-person brainstorm. Write words or phrases that come to mind on the topic or people you need to speak about. Don't discount anything. Get it all down as what appears a hare-brained idea could spark off a better one.

The longer you spend capturing thoughts and ideas, the better you will feel. As you get your ideas on paper, you will start to see patterns or themes to link together. Don't expect answers to come to you immediately. Just be happy to collect together thoughts, ideas, examples, questions, websites, quotations, case studies, diagrams, charts, pictures, and anecdotes. The more widely you think and read, the more likely you are to be struck by inspiration.

But the best source of material could be *you*. If you're giving a speech or presentation, you may already know a lot about the bride and groom, the community housing project, the dearly deceased, the client proposal, or whatever you need to talk about. The best speeches often stem from a personal perspective. An audience is more likely to engage with a speaker who talks from the heart. Use the following questions to create a unique starting point for your speech:

- What's your personal experience of the topic (or person you're speaking about)?
- What frustrates you about this topic?
- What do you enjoy about it?
- What's the weirdest/saddest/funniest/stupidest thing you ever heard about this topic?
- What do (or would) your grandparents or a 5-year-old child think about it?

It could be an interesting twist to start your speech with what you used to believe about marriage when you were 6 years old. Or to begin by sharing what your grandmother would make of your company's financial difficulties.

3 Craft your speech structure

Right, you have a bunch of examples, ideas, and anecdotes that you want to talk about. Next you need to assemble them in an order that helps your audience to make sense of them. Imagine if someone presents you with the letters H E P S E and C. Doesn't make sense, does it? But now consider if they were presented in the order S P E E C H.

Think about these ways to order your speech.

- **A chronological order.** Talk about what happened in the past, what's happening in the present, and then what could or should happen in the future. A chronological order is straightforward and you won't lose anyone as you give your talk.

- **An acronym or word.** This can provide a structure to what otherwise seems a random collection of ideas. SWOT is a popular word for talking through strengths and weaknesses, opportunities and threats. But why not create your own? For example, 'I'll talk you through the SURE model – the Scale of the problem, its Urgency, our Response, and I'll finish by Eliciting questions.' Or here's another one I made up: FEAR – 'I'll talk about the Feasibility of this project, how we Engage our employees, the Actions we need to take, and the Research we must conduct with customers.' Go on, have a go at creating your own mnemonic.

- **Theory followed by practice.** Start with the theory and then describe the practice. For example, 'The theory about marriage is that you find someone you love and then propose. But I'm going to tell you the horrible truth about what happened to John and Laura in practice!'

- **Problem followed by solution.** State a problem, then guide your audience to the solution. For example, 'I'm going to describe the three problems that are causing us financial grief then talk about possible solutions for tackling each of them.'

Don't forget about visual aids. Having something for people to look at while they listen to you is a great way to take some of the pressure off you. Be as daring or conservative as you like – visual aids can be whatever you want. Projecting slides onto a screen can draw the audience's attention away from you and remind you what to say. You could whip out a poster-sized photo of the birthday boy or girl aged 18 months to a round of 'ahhhh'. You could brandish a copy of your company's annual report as you talk about the pressures that your team faces.

4 Add an introduction and a conclusion

There's a famous saying about how to give presentations: 'Tell them what you're gonna tell them; tell them; then tell them what you told them.' In other words, start your presentation with a brief introduction, an overview of the key points you will discuss. In the main body of your presentation, you discuss those main points in more depth, perhaps illustrating them with facts, examples, or anecdotes. Finally, you end with a conclusion summarising your main points.

Your introduction is particularly important. Remember that first impressions do count. So the first words that come out of your mouth are particularly important. When I run presentation skills courses for companies, I always suggest to the people I'm training that they should commit to memory at least the first couple of minutes of their presentations. It's fine to use notes for the main body of your presentation, but make an effort to learn your introduction so you can come across as smooth and confident in those vital first few minutes.

5 Practise, practise, practise!

Psychologists talk about the need to practise 'outputting' as well as 'inputting' a speech. Sitting quietly and reading your notes (inputting) pushes it into your brain. But you need to practise speaking it out loud (outputting) so you can pull it out of your brain too.

But I'm not talking about any old way to speak it out loud. They say that practice makes perfect, but I disagree. Because only *perfect* practice makes perfect performance on the big day. The more you simulate the conditions in which you need to give your speech, the more you will get out of your practice. If the actual presentation needs to be delivered while standing up, then stand while you practise. Project the slides behind you if you're using them. Rehearse out loud and at the right volume as if a packed audience is in front of you. And remember to speak slowly and deeply (see the section 'Sounding confident: when less is more' in Chapter 3).

It's up to you how much you want to rely on notes. Read your notes if you need to do it that way – even famous business leaders, presidents, and prime ministers sometimes read out their speeches. But practise your speech enough so that you don't have to rely on notes for every word. If you look up occasionally and make eye contact with your audience, you show that you know what you're talking about. Even better if you can reduce your notes down to a handful of bullet points on a sheet of paper. Every time you run through your speech, you will learn a bit more and need to rely on your notes a little less. If you want to be good, be sure to practise. If you want to be great, practise a lot.

6 Pile on the pressure

To get the most out of your practice, I suggest that you rehearse at least once or twice in front of a live audience. For a big, important presentation, aim to get a handful of your colleagues or friends together to hear you speak. Even if your audience consists of only a single person – perhaps someone you live with, a friend, or a colleague, you will get lots out of it. It doesn't matter if they know anything about the topic you're speaking about. The point is simply to rehearse in front of a live audience. Presenting in front of actual people will help you to get used to being scrutinised while you speak; it will take the edge off for the big day itself.

You may have to bribe your audience to sit and listen to your talk. Buy them something to eat while you give your speech. Offer to do the household chores in exchange for a half-hour of their time. If your presentation is really long, perhaps ask your friends to listen to just the first half-hour or only the introduction.

Trust me. Practising out loud to a live audience will allow you to relax much more when you come to deliver the real thing.

7 Check that you will RISE to the occasion

As you practise your presentation or speech, you may find yourself tweaking what you want to say. Sometimes, what we think will sound interesting or impressive doesn't sound quite as good when we rehearse it out loud. When I run presentation skills courses (and feel free to invite me – rob@talentspace.co.uk – to your organisation to run one for you and your colleagues!) I say that the four letters that make up RISE are possibly the most important check you need to perform on your material:

■ **Relevance**. Make sure that the facts, information or even sentiments you wish to share are relevant to this particular audience. Sometimes, as an expert, we know more than our audience. But good presenters make sure that their content is targeted precisely at each particular audience's interests and needs.

■ **Insight**. If you only want your audience to remember one key message, what would it be? We can sometimes be guilty of putting together presentations that bombard our audiences with too much information. So make sure that you are certain about the key insight(s) that you wish to get across.

■ **Stories.** The best presentations tend to use stories, anecdotes and personal examples to bring the material to life. As a rule of thumb, I suggest having around one story for every 10 to 15 minutes of your presentation to retain the interest of your audience.

■ **Enthusiasm.** Remember that a presentation or speech isn't just about conveying facts. If people only wanted facts, you could simply send them a handout with a transcript of what you intend to say. So when you practise, make sure that you're presenting with enthusiasm about the topic.

8 Sort out the practical stuff

Having something go wrong on the big day itself won't do much for your confidence. So it pays to think ahead. To ensure that your speech goes smoothly, consider the following:

■ Do you know exactly where the venue is and how to get there? Don't arrive dripping with sweat because you didn't leave enough time and had to sprint up three flights of stairs to find the right room!

■ Are you happy with the audiovisual equipment? Do you know how to operate the microphone, laptop, slide projector? And who can help if it breaks down?

■ Do you know where the toilets are for that last-minute comfort break?

■ Can you get a glass of water in case your mouth goes dry?

9 Calm your mind and body

Even when we know our material, the voice in our heads – that darned inner critic – can still torture our thoughts. However, these four Confidence Boosters are especially powerful for tackling pre-speech worries.

- Well before your speech, start visualising success (see 'Confidence Booster: Using the movie screen in your head' on pages 48–9) to get your mind used to the idea that you can do it.

- If you experience stabs of panic about speaking, use the FACADe technique (see 'Confidence Booster: Giving form to your thoughts' on page 36). Challenge the automatic negative thoughts (ANTs) in your head and you will see that many of your worries are unrealistic.

- Prior to the big day, create capability-affirming thoughts (see 'Confidence Booster: Creating your cool CATs' on page 31) to repeat in the final minutes before you deliver your speech. Or use the ABCD technique (see 'Confidence Booster: Calming your emotions with ABCD' on pages 56–7). Whichever one you use is entirely down to personal preference and what works best for you.

- A half-hour or so before your speech, find an empty office, dressing room, or even toilet cubicle and do a vocal warm-up (see 'Confidence Booster: Performing vocal gymnastics' on page 66). And check that you are breathing in a natural, relaxed fashion too (see 'Confidence Booster: Diaphragmatic breathing' on page 55).

10 Be entertaining *and* educational

OK, time to step up and deliver what you need to say. This final step is a reminder that all audiences are looking not only to be informed but also entertained. No matter how dry or technical your topic, you can make it more enjoyable by allowing your personality to come through. So smile, use hand gestures to illustrate key points, and think about your body language (see Chapter 3). If you look like you're having a good time, your audience is more likely to have one too.

Also bear in mind that even great presenters sometimes stumble over their words, have problems with slide projectors, get their facts wrong occasionally, and so on. Thankfully, audiences have short attention spans and are often too wrapped up in their own thoughts to let minor slip-ups register for long. No matter what mistakes you make, you can be certain that most of your audience will have forgotten about them by the next morning! So be proud of yourself for doing something that a lot of other people can't or won't do.

Finally, rest assured that your audience probably can't tell if you don't *feel* very confident. Sure, you can feel your heart racing, your dry mouth, and the sweat on your palms. But your audience can't see any of those. If it helps, bring to mind the persona of someone else you know who seems to behave with confidence all of the time. Pretend to be that person for the duration of your presentation. As long as you present *as if* you're a confident presenter, you will do a great job!

09

Confident conversations and socialising

Ever been to a party or social occasion and felt self-conscious, not knowing who to talk to or what to say? Well, you're not alone. Many people worry about social situations such as striking up conversations with people. Even people you know who *appear* to be the life and soul of the party can feel insecure on the inside when venturing into unknown social territory.

Most folks would like to meet new people and make friends. But just because we crave social contact doesn't mean that we are automatically good at it. Fortunately, social skill is precisely that – it's a *skill*. Professor Bernardo Carducci at the Shyness Research Institute at Indiana University has interviewed thousands of people who experience shyness and he believes that no one is born shy. Which means that social confidence can be taught, practised, and honed. So let's cover 10 straightforward tactics enabling you to get more out of socialising.

1 Know what you're getting into

Our fears are often greatest when we don't know what we're letting ourselves in for. So pick up the telephone and speak to your host, or do a little planning to make sure a social occasion goes well. Here are some questions to think through:

- What time does the event start and where will it be held? A good tip is to get there on time. Many parties don't get busy until later. If you're nervous about meeting strangers, arriving early means you can be personally introduced to a few people before the crowds appear.

- What do you need to take along? Should you bring a bottle or flowers or some other gift? Whip up a culinary creation or bring a store-bought dessert?

- Who else will be there? Could you bring a friend to keep you company? If you feel nervous about social occasions, find a friend who is adept at social chit-chat to provide moral support.

- What are you going to wear? Looking good outwardly can help you to feel more confident inwardly. Plan ahead rather than risk discovering at the last minute that your favourite outfit is stained or hasn't been ironed.

2 Be an active listener, not talker

A lot of people get nervous socially because they don't like being scrutinised by others. They worry that others will be looking and laughing at them. But the reality is that most people are too concerned about themselves to be thinking about you. And you can turn this fact to your advantage.

In most social situations, people gravitate towards folks who are 'good listeners'. In other words, most people like to talk about themselves. So ask other people about themselves – even the waiter. Once people get talking, you'll feel less tense.

What questions could you ask people? The next time you find yourself with friends, make a mental note of the questions that people ask each other. Or make a comment about what's going on around you – the event, activity, or your general surroundings – and turn it into a question. 'I've never been in this restaurant before – have you?' or 'It's a gorgeous evening, isn't it?'

Of course I'm not suggesting that you fire questions at people irrespective of where the conversation is going – that's an interrogation, not a conversation. But if there is a lull in the conversation, having a few questions at the ready means you can always get the banter going again. Common ice breakers include open-ended questions such as:

- 'How do you know the host?' or 'What brings you to this event?'
- 'What do you do for a living?'
- 'How has your morning/day/week been so far?'

3 Show that you're listening and interested

Most people are more than happy to talk about themselves. But it helps if you can show that you're interested with both your body language and what you say. Imagine if you were talking to them and they were looking out of the window, rolling their eyes and shaking their heads continually! Be sure to look the other person in the eyes when they're talking. Nod occasionally to show that you understand and maybe even empathise with what they're saying. Avoid crossing your hands over your chest (which can seem dismissive or even angry!) and remember to smile when it's appropriate to show you're having a good time.

Once you've got someone talking, you can encourage them to talk further by dropping in comments and observations. Show that you're listening with responses such as 'It sounds like your daughter is great fun' or 'You must be very motivated to go running even when it's raining!'

To continue the conversation, ask open-ended questions rather than closed questions that could just be answered with a 'yes' or 'no'. For example, asking 'What do you most enjoy about your job?' is better than 'Do you enjoy your job?' (which could just be answered with a 'no', ending the conversation!) Similarly, 'What do you like to do outside of work?' is better than 'Do you follow a football team?' or 'Do you have holiday plans?' (which could again both be answered with a conversation-killing 'no').

4 Have something to say

Whenever I ask one particular friend how he is, he always replies 'Mustn't grumble.' I've even told him off for saying that, because it puts an immediate downer on the conversation. All I hear is the word 'grumble', which makes me feel like the conversation is going to be hard work.

When I ask another friend 'What have you been up to?' she replies with 'Not a lot.' Again, it kills the conversation dead.

Whether you're talking to a group at a party or a single person on a date, you can't bombard them with questions. You need to talk about yourself as well. Psychologists call it the principle of *reciprocity* – both parties in a conversation have to make a contribution. If you ask people what they do for a living, be ready for them to ask what you do too. But the secret here is to give an answer that encourages other people either to ask further questions or to talk about their lives further.

So avoid giving one-word or overly short answers. Rather than saying 'I'm an accountant', how about 'I studied geography at university but somehow I ended up becoming an accountant What do you do?' or 'Technically speaking I'm an accountant, but really I consider myself a frustrated artist. What's your secret passion?' Such answers combine self-disclosure, which builds rapport, with a question to return the conversational ball into the other person's court.

Or if someone asks you where you live, don't say 'Clapham'. Try 'Clapham, quite a distance from the nearest train station but really close to a little bakery that sells amazing cranberry muffins'. That contains prompts such as 'train station', 'bakery' and 'muffins', allowing multiple avenues for your conversational partner to pursue.

How would *you* answer the following common questions?

- 'Any plans to go away on holiday?'
- 'Following anything in particular on the telly?'
- 'What do you like doing outside of work?'
- 'Seen any good films/read any good books lately?'

Don't learn responses off-by-heart. But at least have a rough idea of how you could reply to the more common questions that people ask. Just a little preparation will mean you can keep the conversation flowing when you're in the thick of it.

5 Use positive body language

Look as if you're having a good time and you will draw other people to you. Look like you're shy or anxious and of course people will worry about engaging with you. Chapter 3 covers body language extensively and how to behave as if you already possess confidence. But as a quick reminder:

- **Smile and make eye contact**. People notice facial expressions long before they notice your clothes, hair, and so on. People are drawn to smiles – even month-old babies can recognise a smile and respond positively to it. And remember that smiling causes changes in the brain that can make you feel happier too – even if at first you don't feel it.

- **Check your posture and use of hands**. If you let your shoulders slump and have your arms crossed, you send the message that you don't like to talk to people. Stand tall, keep your chin up, and avoid making jerky, awkward movements.

When you're chatting, use a technique called 'active listening' to demonstrate that you are paying attention to what's being said. Nod your head occasionally in agreement with what people say. Use words and noises such as 'yes', 'uh-huh', and 'go on' to signal audibly that you're listening. And allow appropriate expressions to cross your face too – a smile for a funny story, a serious face if someone tells you about a difficult situation, or surprise if someone tells you something unexpected.

6 Know what's going on in the world

When we meet people for the first time, we often engage in fairly superficial banter or 'small talk' about the weather, what's on TV, or events that have happened in the world at large.

Obviously, no one wants to look ignorant. So make sure to spend a little time every day checking on what's happening in the news and media in general. Years ago, I used to recommend that people buy a newspaper on the day of any social occasion. But now we have the Internet. As little as five minutes online should be enough to give you a broad appreciation of what's going on in both national and world news as well as popular culture. My personal must-read destination is the BBC's website (http://news.bbc.co.uk) but you may find your own favourites.

I'm not suggesting that you spend hours poring over what's happening in the world. However, just a passing familiarity with the big stories of the day may be enough for you to talk briefly about them with a conversational partner.

7 Be yourself

Managing your outward appearance to mask your initial lack of confidence is a good thing. But pretending to be someone other than yourself is not.

Sure, we bond with people by finding common ground. But that only works if you genuinely share the same passion. Feign interest when you know nothing about a topic and you show yourself up as a fraud.

Part of confident socialising is being comfortable with what you're good or not so good at. If someone asks you about your favourite football team, soap opera, Man Booker prize-nominated novel, or whatever, be honest. Admit that you don't know anything about it and either show a polite interest (e.g. 'I don't really follow the soaps – do you have a favourite?') or change the topic (e.g. 'I'm more a fan of thrillers myself – what else do you enjoy doing with your time?').

Don't try to be all things to all people. You'll come across better talking about what you actually know and enjoy.

8 Focus your attention outwards

When you feel nervous, you may focus more on what's going on inside your head than what's going on around you. But focusing on what your inner critic says can get distracting when you should be listening to the people around you. However, you can use the principles of mindfulness (see 'Confidence Booster: Becoming mindful' on pages 128–9) not only to calm yourself down but also to focus on other people rather than your own thoughts.

Essentially, becoming more mindful is simply about choosing what you focus on. You probably already do this some of the time anyway. If you're on the telephone but the TV is on, you can switch your attention to the speaker down the line rather than the television next to you. Or if you're at work and people are chatting around you, you can either choose to listen in or focus on what you're supposed to be doing.

Becoming more mindful when you're out and about is pretty much the same thing. But this time you are choosing to direct the spotlight of your attention away from the niggling voice in your head and on to the person talking to you.

Make a concerted effort to listen to what people are saying and doing. Avoid evaluating what's going on. If you notice thoughts cropping up such as 'Oh no, I can't believe I said that!', let them go. Trust yourself to speak without judging everything you say.

Research shows that most people usually pay only about half as much attention to you as you think they do. So remember that you'll be judging your comments much more harshly than the people around you will be.

9 Get fired up

Capability-affirming thoughts (see 'Confidence Booster: Creating your cool CATs on page 31) are great for staying positive. Put in the time well before the day of the party or social event so you can decide on some positive statements to buoy up your confidence. CATs that have worked for other people include:

- 'It's OK to be nervous but I can keep my nerves in check.'
- 'I'm a good listener.'
- 'Focus on the person I'm talking to.'
- 'I'm going to approach someone and say hello.'
- 'Lots of people feel nervous but I want to enjoy myself.'

Decide on your own CATs and repeat them under your breath or in your head on the way to the event. And when you have finished one conversation and are about to start the next, take the opportunity to remind yourself of them.

Remember to look after your body too. Be aware of your breathing (see 'Confidence Booster: Diaphragmatic breathing' on page 55) to ensure you help yourself to breathe naturally and calmly. Or use the ABCD technique (see 'Confidence Booster: Calming your emotions with ABCD' on pages 56–7).

All it takes is a little preparation and a few basic techniques. Soon you will supercharge your social life!

10 Practise on strangers

Becoming more confident at chatting to people isn't something that we can only practise at parties and other big social occasions. Most of us encounter many people every single day without really thinking about it. When you buy a train ticket or get your groceries scanned at a supermarket checkout, you are interacting with another human being. So why not take that opportunity to hone your social skills by striking up a short conversation?

Make an effort to see the world from that person's perspective for a moment. Smile, then say hello and ask a question or make a comment that's relevant to them. For example, if you're buying a train ticket, you could say 'Hello. Bet you're glad that rush hour is over now. How has your morning been so far?' If you're at the supermarket checkout, you might remark on one of the items you've bought: 'I had this dessert last week and I couldn't resist getting another one. Have you tried it?'

More often than not, you'll find that most people are more than happy to engage in a few seconds of chit-chat. On occasion, you may come across a slightly quieter person – perhaps they're at the end of a long shift and tired or just rather shy and uncommunicative. But that's OK, you're not trying to make lifelong friends, only to practise starting up conversations.

Set yourself a target. Perhaps to engage at least one or two people in a brief conversation every day. And all the while, you will be honing your ability to socialise and have confident conversations.

Confident dating

If you're reading this chapter, I think it's safe to assume that you might like to ask someone out, enjoy dating, and perhaps find The One. Often, what holds people back from success at dating isn't anything innate. It's definitely not the case that some people are born to be successful at dating and being in relationships. Most of what may be holding you back is probably in your head. The good news though is that we can remove those blocks and help you to get more out of dating and relationships. Here are 10 tips on how to do it.

1 Realise that you've everything to gain

So you'd like to go on a date but don't have the confidence to ask someone out (or say 'yes' to someone who might ask you out). Rest assured that you're not alone. But, if you think it through, you'll see that you really should ask that person out. You have nothing to lose and *everything* to gain.

If you ask someone out, you may meet someone fun and entertaining. That person could become someone special in your life or turn into a new close friend. You might have a beautiful romance. You could end up getting married or living together. You might have lots of passionate sex. You might build a home together. Having children or travelling the world together could be possibilities too. In fact, who knows what might happen? There's almost unlimited upside to asking someone out or at least saying 'yes' when someone asks you out.

But that can only happen if you decide to ask someone out. If you don't, then you will never know what might happen (if you lack confidence initiating conversations with people, see tip number 10 in Chapter 9 on 'Confident conversations and socialising' to build your confidence gradually).

Of course, you may be worried about the downside of asking someone out. You hate the idea of being rejected, but rejection can't kill you. And if someone says 'no', what have you actually lost? Nothing. That person wasn't in your life beforehand and they're still not in your life now. At least now you know that person isn't interested so you can move on.

Towards the end of their lives, more people regret what they *didn't* do than what they did. Don't get to the end of your life and regret that you never took a chance.

2 Get used to saying 'yes'

A single friend of mine says quite categorically that he will not do online dating. I think that's a shame. Because at least four other friends of ours have met some great people online. Two of those friends are now in long-term relationships with people they met from the Internet too. And all because they were willing to try something new. When they came across the idea of online dating, they said 'yes'.

I'm not saying that you must do online dating. No. The point is simply that you should say 'yes' to more opportunities. Avoid closing your mind to anything. You never know when romance might blossom.

Join clubs, societies, evening classes, drama groups, sports teams, anything and everything. One thing is certain: you won't meet anyone by staying at home. When someone invites you to a party, say 'yes'. Doesn't matter if you don't think you'll know anyone. You might just make a new friend who could ultimately introduce you to someone who is right for you. Or if a friend invites you to go bowling or hiking or salsa dancing or whatever else, just do it, say 'yes'.

Ignore any preconceptions you may have and instead just accept the offers you get. If you listen to stories on the radio or read about how people met their partners, you'll notice that they often got together in all sorts of unusual or even downright bizarre situations. So get used to saying 'yes'.

3 Look good to feel good

If you want to be attractive, you have to feel good about yourself. So think about how you dress yourself. Now, society and the media place a lot of emphasis on how we look. Women are supposed to look slim and pretty; men are required to look handsome and hunky. But let me make it clear that I'm *not* suggesting that you alter yourself to conform to the media's unrealistic expectations of how either women or men should look.

What I'm talking about is making sure that you're confident with your appearance and how you dress. When you feel confident about what's on the outside, you will feel more confident on the inside. If you haven't been on the dating scene in a while, you may have gotten used to wearing certain items that feel comfortable ('why make the effort?') and saving your best clothes for special occasions. But why wait? Make every day special by wearing what makes you feel most confident about yourself.

So throw away those tattered old clothes. You know the ones. Remember that this isn't about trying to conform to whatever is currently considered fashionable; this is only about ensuring you feel good about yourself. So go through every item in your wardrobe and ask yourself: 'Does this make me *feel* confident?' If not, bin it and perhaps treat yourself to something new (see also 'Take Action: Dressing for success' on pages 62–3).

4 Keep it simple

The media feeds us a lot of rubbish about what a 'date' should be like. We tend to have an image of two people dressed smartly, chatting over a lavish dinner, with perhaps soft music playing in the background and a candle glowing gently on the table. But that doesn't have to be what modern dating is about.

Sure, that's *one* way of having a date. But if you're still finding your way on the dating scene, it's a rather high-pressure way of going on a date. So much has to go right for that romantic mood and you may end up spending more time worrying about the food and the music and the setting than on simply enjoying each other's company. So take the pressure off instead.

Suggest that you go for a drink after work or a coffee at the weekend. Just two people in a pub or a coffee shop having a chat. It's simple to organise and there's less pressure. And when you feel less weight of expectation, you will feel more relaxed, more confident.

5 Remember that even a date is still a conversation

Sure, going on a date may be a bit more nerve-wracking than merely chatting to a friend or talking to a stranger at a party. But a date is still ultimately a conversation between two people. Chapter 9 covers 10 essentials for confident conversations and socialising. So make sure you apply those principles.

But here are a few extra tips:

■ Compliment your date on how he or she looks. Most people put a bit of effort into choosing what to wear on a date and it's nice to know that it paid off. You don't have to make the compliment immediately when you get together. Take your time to decide on something you *genuinely* like about the other person's clothing or perhaps how they've styled their hair, and drop it into the conversation later on.

■ Try to keep the conversation upbeat and interesting. Talking about a terrible earthquake or famine overseas may be topical, but it's not exactly date material. Ask your date questions about how they like to spend their time. And be ready to share interesting or amusing stories about yourself too.

■ Look for topics on which you can both agree. This is a date, not a debate. People tend to be attracted to people who have similar views. Arguing over your political beliefs, the existence of God, or other contentious topics won't help you to build a rapport and establish the mutual attraction.

6 Steer clear of your personal minefield

The early stages of dating are similar to a job interview. On an interview, the interviewer is scoping you out to decide whether to offer you a permanent position. On a date, you're both scoping each other out and deciding whether to enter into what could ultimately become a permanent role too.

When you're on an interview, you don't tell the interviewer all of your inner secrets, everything that's bad about you and the reasons you left all of the jobs you had. No, that would scare off an interviewer. So don't do it on a date either.

When you go out with someone – even when it's for the second or third time – remember that you're still dating. This is the very earliest stages of a relationship, not a TV talk show in which you're being encouraged to talk about all of your ex-partners, why things went wrong, the reasons you're unattached, or anything else bad about yourself. By all means talk about your interests: your favourite books, films, TV programmes, hobbies, friends and places to visit. But avoid talking about the bad stuff, any periods of ill-health, deaths in the family, how much you hate your job, or the painful break-ups you had.

If you're carrying any relationship baggage with you, think of a way to deflect the conversation. So what would be a positive spin to put on your situation should your date ask you about your dating history? Rather than saying 'He/she dumped me for my best friend two years ago and I've not had the confidence to go out with anyone until now' perhaps say 'I split up from my ex a couple of years ago – I won't go into the detail – and now I feel quite positive and open about the idea of meeting someone new.'

So how might you talk about your past in more positive terms?

7 Signal your interest with body language

One of the differences between a date versus a mere conversation with a friend or stranger is that you're probably attracted to your date and would like to take things further. But in the early stages of a date, it's inappropriate to make overly aggressive statements such as: 'I am attracted to you and want to have sex with you' or 'I know we've only known each other for a couple of hours, but I can already see you being the father of the children I'd like to have.'

No. Dating is much more subtle. In Chapter 3, I talked about how to convey confidence through your body language. But now it's time to think about how we convey the fact that we're attracted to someone through our non-verbal communication. And we do that through touch.

So look for ways to get into physical contact with your date – although of course this has to be in *appropriate* ways. When you greet each other, make sure you at least give your date a kiss on the cheek (or two if you're feeling European). Perhaps give your date a squeeze around the shoulders or look for a subtle way to touch your date on the upper arm as you walk towards the bar or restaurant. When you're sitting near each other, find a way to brush fingers, perhaps as you pass him or her a drink. Dancing is a great way to build rapport and establish a connection because you're usually clasping hands or putting a hand on your partner's waist or shoulder.

For the first few dates, make sure that your date doesn't get the wrong impression and think that you're only interested in being friends. Use the psychology of interpersonal contact to send the message that you'd like to take things further.

8 Convey your interest with words too

While signalling your interest through your body language and physical touch is a good start, that's not all you need to do. Physical contact is still quite a subtle way to get the point across – and not everyone can read the signals correctly. So you need to convey your interest with words too.

Remember that your thoughts exist only in your head. When I've observed friends who are dating, they often make statements like 'It's so obvious I like him' or 'She can't possibly know that I'm not attracted to her.' But people are often oblivious to how other people feel about them. The only way to make sure someone knows you want to see them again is by saying so.

When a date is over, send a text or email or call. I'd leave it until the next morning so as not to appear too keen (unless he or she gets in touch first, then it's only polite to reply). Say something positive about why you enjoyed the date and end with a phrase like 'I'd like to do that again – are you free on Friday?' or 'I had a fabulous time but next time you'll have to let me pay.'

Don't make the people you date have to guess whether you like them or not!

9 Enjoy dating for what it is

Try to enjoy dating. Dating isn't only about the destination; it can also be about the journey. Yes, your goal may be to meet someone special, perhaps to settle down with The One. But you can enjoy the journey too. You're meeting new people, socialising with stimulating individuals, and learning about them and the world around you. Some of the people you date might become friends. A few of your dates might turn into interesting anecdotes that you can later laugh about with your friends!

When you take the pressure off yourself of trying to meet The One, you'll find that you relax more, enjoy yourself more, and come across as more confident and attractive. And *that* is when romance is most likely to strike.

10 Learn and move on

Only in the movies do couples lock eyes with each other, know that they are destined to be together, fall deeply, madly and passionately in love, and stroll into the sunset together to live happily ever after. For the rest of us mere mortals, dating is a fairly hit and miss affair. The reality is that most of us have to kiss a few frogs before we find our prince or princess. Nearly all of my friends – and probably most of the people you know too – have been on more than a few dates, had a few boyfriends or girlfriends, and went on a few more dates before they settled into a relationship.

People split up, get dumped, or decide things aren't working all the time. So accept that rejection is a part of dating. Two things though. First, keep your spirits up. Realise that it happens to everyone (we've all been interested in someone but been rejected or dumped). The STRAIN technique is quite good for getting over rejection (see 'Confidence Booster: Taking the

STRAIN out' on pages 143–4) and so is the FACADe if you're feeling particularly low (see 'Confidence Booster: Giving form to your thoughts' on page 36). Second, figure out what you can learn from your dates. What can you learn and what could you do better next time?

But avoid beating yourself up over the rejection. Remember that everyone gets rejected occasionally. So imagine a compassionate friend reviewing what happened. In fact, a good tip is to bring to mind your most supportive, most compassionate friend. What's his or her name? Hear in your mind his or her voice asking you the following questions:

- What went well? What should you continue to do in future?
- What could have been better? What will you do differently on a future date?

Review your dates with a positive, compassionate mindset and you will get better with every date you go on.

11

Confident meetings at work and networking

Ever heard the saying 'It's not *what* you know, it's *who* you know'? It's true that working relationships play a big part in creating business success. Perhaps you want to state your case for a pay rise to your boss or need to give a colleague hard-hitting criticism about their performance. Maybe you are aiming to negotiate a business deal or simply network with as many new contacts as possible. Whatever you need, it comes down to building effective relationships with people.

Winning over colleagues and clients in business meetings isn't rocket science. As with much in life, a little planning and preparation go a long way. To allow you to be your best at work, I share with you my top 10 tips for confident encounters at work.

1 Decide on your objective

You need to know what you want out of a meeting or encounter. Do you want to raise your profile in the team, network with prospective clients at a conference, or sign up a new customer?

Whatever you want, write it down. Having a clear objective will help you to be more focused and productive in working towards what you want.

2 Get used to wearing other people's shoes

Business success is about relationships. And to create strong relationships, you need to see all of your interactions through the eyes of other people. Imagine that you're meeting with your boss. What do you think your boss would rather hear – a list of what you're not happy with or suggestions as to how you can make the team more successful? Or if you're meeting with a customer, do you think the customer is more interested in your company's history or how you can save her organisation time and money?

Imagine that you're tuned into the radio station WII-FM. Imagine a big sign on the forehead of everyone you meet that says: 'What's in it for me?' Sure, you have an objective, but you need to find a way to make your approaches genuinely interesting for other people. Put yourself into their shoes to answer the question and you will get far. Get used to behaving generously towards other people and you may find that they can't help but help you in turn.

3 Ask what you can do for others

Putting ourselves into the shoes of other people is a good start. But the best way to figure out what other people want is to ask them. I'm not suggesting that you will necessarily be able to help out every single person you encounter, but it doesn't hurt to ask. You could ask all of the people you meet when you're networking at conferences. Perhaps do it for the handful of key people you interact with on a regular basis. And you should certainly do it for your boss.

Remember that your boss has his or her own projects and worries to think about. If you want to get noticed for the right reasons, ask your boss what he or she is working on and what you could do to contribute. By doing so, you demonstrate to your boss that you're not just focused on the tasks that you have to do, but also aware of the bigger picture at work. And that's the kind of helpful attitude that ultimately gets people promoted.

When you can help other people, they become indebted to you. Once they owe you a favour or two, you can then ask for whatever you want.

4 Create your spoken logo

Business etiquette usually dictates that you introduce yourself with a hello and your name. No surprises so far. But then you may get asked 'What do you do?' It pays dividends to give some thought to your answer, the 'blurb' or spoken logo you use to introduce yourself. Simply saying 'I'm a teacher' or 'I run a business that creates online advertising' may be accurate. But is it exciting? Does it whet the appetite of the people you talk to and make them want to find out more?

A client of mine says with a cheeky smile: 'I make business people famous' rather than simply saying he works in public relations. I could say 'I'm a coaching psychologist', but that's a bit yawn-inducing. So I tell people 'I'm a TV psychologist'. Even though I don't spend all of my time on television, it's more exciting and encourages people to ask questions and want to know more.

Think about creating a spoken logo that is appropriate to your audience and your objective. If you want to be taken seriously, you need to make weightier comments about yourself. If you want to capture the interest of people who might not otherwise be interested, think about a quirkier phrase to use. How could you describe yourself in a way that is more exciting than your mere job title? And always remember to introduce yourself with a smile to make yourself come across as approachable and someone that others will want to talk to.

5 See what works – and what doesn't

They say that there's no need to reinvent the wheel and they're right. Why struggle to find out the best way to do everything when great examples of it are going on all around you?

Look at your colleagues and acquaintances. Pick the ones who get it right most of the time. What is it that they say or do? Is it a phrase or a way with words that you could adapt for your own use? Is it their manner as they enter a room and shake hands with everyone present?

Watch also the colleagues who aren't held in very high regard. What mistakes or *faux pas* do they commit? What do they do (or not do) that causes others to shun them?

People have always learned by observation, learning from their successes and steering clear of their mistakes. You may need to watch other people on a couple of occasions; perhaps capture your thoughts in a journal. But certainly don't be scared to expand your repertoire by learning from others. Looking and listening is one of the most powerful tools available to us to accelerate our confidence in all sorts of business situations (see 'Take Action: Learning from the best' on page 58 for further guidance on making a good impression in work situations).

6 Remember that people can only notice what you say and do

Are you the kind of person who tends not to say a lot during meetings? You probably prefer to speak up only when you have something of genuine value to add. You may even disapprove of the kind of people who speak up in meetings just for the sake of being noticed. Unfortunately, research suggests that you may need to speak up more if you want to do well in your career.

Research psychologist Cameron Anderson at the University of California, Berkeley found that people in meetings tend to rate the people who speak up the most during meetings as both cleverer and more creative than people who don't say as much. Remember that the people around you can only judge you on what you do and say. They can't see into your head. They can't tell how smart you are unless you speak up and share your thoughts during meetings.

So speak up. Say what's on your mind. I'm not suggesting that you should try to dominate meetings by talking nonsense. Just try to be a little more involved. For example, you might be able to contribute by paraphrasing what's been said to clarify what people agree or disagree about. Or, when the group is stuck with a knotty problem, ask open-ended questions such as 'What other options could we consider?' or 'Have we ever encountered a similar problem before?'

If you find it tough to think on your feet, do a little planning before you go into a meeting. What points might you raise or questions might you ask to add to the discussion? Jot down even a handful of bullet points about what you might say and you give yourself a better shot at sounding intelligent should you get the chance to speak.

7 Focus on relationships as well as tasks

Few people enjoy meetings. Most of us would rather get on with what we think we should be doing rather than sit in meetings. But if you want to do well at work, I humbly suggest that you may actually need to initiate *more* meetings.

The problem with most meetings is that there are too many people fighting to talk at once. If you're a more reserved sort who doesn't like to have to shout over other people, you probably don't get enough of a chance to get your point across. So try initiating more *one-to-one* meetings.

If there are important colleagues or major customers that you need to talk to, try to get time with each of them on their own. Suggest that the two of you meet for an informal coffee or that you share a quick sandwich lunch together. If the people you need to meet are pressed for time, as little as ten or even five minutes may sometimes be enough to exchange views and talk through the issues you both have. Do it and you'll find that having occasional one-to-one discussions will not only help you to get your point across but also help you to understand each of your colleagues and customers better too.

8 Turn your objective into a SPOT goal

I mentioned at the start of this chapter that it helps to have an objective. But in Chapter 4 I talked about how a SPOT goal is even better to keep you motivated. Only when you have a goal that is stretching and significant, positive, observable, and timed can you know at the end of a business encounter whether you have succeeded or need to work harder next time to achieve your goal. Here are some examples of work-related SPOT goals:

■ 'I will introduce myself to 12 new people before we break for lunch.'

■ 'I will speak up and make at least four contributions in this next meeting.'

■ 'By the end of the meeting, I will get the client to agree to us making a formal sales presentation to them.'

9 Forge on

Want to secure that promotion or set up your own business? Want to win new customers or come top of the league table? Whatever is driving you, remember that nothing that's worth doing comes immediately.

The important thing is to keep going. Forge on in the face of the occasional setback. You know what they say: 'If at first you don't succeed ...' So use the following exercises and Confidence Boosters when you need a pick-me-up before you try, try again.

■ Make sure you're aware of the resources you have at hand to invigorate yourself. Remind yourself of everything you can use to restore your confidence (see 'Take Action: Tapping your reserves of confidence' on page 114).

■ In your darkest moments, if you feel really down, use the more powerful writing technique to empty your worries and bad feelings on to paper (see 'Confidence Booster: Expressing negative emotions away' on page 154). Then to shift your attention from what's bothering you, use a favourite activity from your list of resources or check what you've saved up in your confidence bank.

■ When you're in the middle of a tough encounter at work, use the CAT technique (see 'Confidence Booster: Creating your cool CATs' on page 31) to keep your inner critic at bay.

10 Review and repeat

Every time you survive an encounter at work, take a few moments to reflect on how it went. Perhaps at the end of the day, take a few minutes to review how you can continue to get better. But take a balanced approach – consider both what went well and what could have been better. A quick way to review how something went is to think about what you want to start, stop, and continue doing. Ask yourself:

■ What should I *start* doing next time that I didn't do this time?

■ What should I *stop* doing that didn't work out so well this time?

■ What worked well that I want to *continue* doing?

Learn what you can and then try again. Action is always better than over-analysis. So go back to your objective and keep working through the 10 tips within this chapter again – only this time even *better* than you did before.

12

Confident job interviews

A lot of people find the make-or-break situation that is an interview a nerve-wracking experience. But it doesn't have to be. *Anyone* can get better at job interviews. No matter when you last had an interview or your previous experience of them, I guarantee that you can do better.

A couple of years ago, the BBC asked me to present a TV series called *How To Get Your Dream Job*. I helped nervous people to do just what the title suggests – to get their dream jobs. Despite their initial lack of confidence, they *all* got better at showcasing their talents in interviews.

When I'm coaching people who are looking for that new job, I always stress that a big part of becoming more confident in interviews is about preparation and practice. When you've put in the hard work, you can go into an interview with the confidence to perform at your best. And I've boiled the essentials down into 10 key steps.

1 Research the role

The first thing to do before an interview is to study the original job advert. Read through it with a highlighter pen and pick out the key words and phrases that tell you what the employer is looking for.

If the advert mentions that the ideal candidate needs to 'schedule appointments for the managing director', you'll need to talk about how you've done that (or something similar) in the past. If the advert states that you need 'a track record of dealing with customers in a professional manner', you can put money on having to explain how you've dealt with different customers during the interview too. Look out also for characteristics such as 'committed', 'outgoing', or 'organised'. You can bet that you'll be asked to talk about why you believe you have those qualities as well.

You'll probably pick out a dozen or so skills and characteristics. Once you've done that, imagine an interviewer asking you the question: 'Give me an example to prove that you have that skill or characteristic.' The next step will help you craft your answers.

2 Bring to mind your successes

Interviewers ask pretty much the same questions over and over again. Even many supposedly new questions end up being mere twists on the same old theme. So rest assured – you don't have to prepare answers to hundreds of questions. All you need to do is think about your key success stories.

A success story is an anecdote about how you have used a skill to make a difference at work. An employer is ultimately looking for someone who can deliver results – so your stories need to explain how you got things done in your current or previous jobs.

Success stories ensure you make a lasting impact on interviewers. Suppose an interviewer asks you 'Are you a good team player?' You could answer 'Yes, I am.' But does that make you memorable? No, not really. But imagine if you shared with the interviewer a success story that goes along the lines of the following: 'Yes I am a good team player. For example, a colleague fell seriously ill and no one else was willing to cover her meetings. So I took it upon myself to cover her workload. For the weeks she was away, I attended about 12 more client meetings than I usually have. I got into work at 8 a.m. every day and worked till past 7 every night. And I went back into the office on Saturday mornings to catch up on paperwork. But the crucial thing was that I didn't let any of our clients down.' Now, *that's* a bit more memorable, right?

Invest in a stock-take of how you have made a difference at work. I suggest that you need around 8 or 10 such stories to cover most scenarios that an interviewer could ask you about. To help you create your stories, use the following questions to prompt your thinking:

- What are you proud of having accomplished at work? Why? What did you specifically do to be so proud of it?

- What skills or talents are you known for at work? Can you think of occasions you demonstrated those?

- Can you think of a time you faced a problem at work and overcame it? What did you do and what was the result?

- When have you dealt with a difficult customer? How did you deal with the situation?

- When have you gone beyond the call of duty? What did you do in that situation?

- When have you been a good team player by helping a colleague out?

- What have you been praised or complimented for at work? What did you do to merit the positive comments?

3 Ace your answers

Interviewers often recycle the same old questions. Here are the top 10 most commonly asked questions:

- 'Tell us a bit about yourself.'

- 'What do you know about our organisation?'

- 'What are your strengths?'

- 'What are your weaknesses?'

- 'Why do you want to work for us?'

- 'Why do you want to leave your current job?'/'Why did you leave your last job?'

- 'Why should we hire you?'

- 'What makes you a stronger candidate than anyone else?'
- 'Where do you see yourself in five years' time?'
- 'Do you have any questions for us?'

Time to get your thinking cap on – jot down at least a few notes on how you would give answers that mention relevant skills, qualities, or experiences in order to impress the interviewers. So, how would you answer these questions?

4 Show your enthusiasm for each particular employer

'Why do you want to work for us?' is one of the trickiest questions to answer. The truth may be that you don't particularly want to work for them. Perhaps you're applying to several companies and you'd be happy to work for any of them. Or you might be tempted to say 'I just need *a* job.'

But employers like to feel special. Every single company in the world feels that they are different to their competitors. So you have to tell the interviewers the answer that they'd *like* to hear. You have to tell them how much you'd like to work for them:

- 'I'm applying for jobs with all of the big accountancy firms, but I'd most like to work for you because ...'
- 'I'm applying for several marketing positions, but you're my first choice because ...'
- 'I've always been interested in retail and I find this organisation fascinating because ...'

Your reasons are up to you. Perhaps you admire their products or the speed of their growth. Perhaps you like the fact that they're a big international firm or a small family-run business. Just do your research and have something to say. Read up about the organisation on the company's website, find out about their competitors, and learn about what this *particular* organisation believes makes it special, different, and better.

5 Prepare to be spontaneous

The more you practise a skill, the better you get at it. And the same goes for giving confident interview responses. Candidates who rehearse giving answers to interview questions always come across better than candidates who don't. This is about doing some preparation beforehand so you can *appear* spontaneous during an interview.

I'm not suggesting that you learn interview answers by rote. What I suggest is that you commit your main points to memory so you can deliver polished responses, *as if* you were speaking off-the-cuff.

You can rehearse your answers on your own. Write out a list of interview questions on a notepad then stab your finger on the notepad to pick one. Or write them on note cards and shuffle them into a random order. Read the question out as if an interviewer has asked it and then give your response. Of course, rehearsing interview answers with a friend can be helpful too. Give your friend a list of questions – or even ask your friend to improvise – so you can practise responding to a live person.

6 Pre-empt those tricky questions

Ever been fired or had a health problem? Ever failed an exam or quit a job after deciding that you hated it? Or maybe you have a disability or haven't worked in a while. Many candidates have one or two issues that they'd rather not talk about. Thing is: simply *hoping* that a topic doesn't come up isn't exactly a great way to feel confident during an interview. Worrying whether the interviewer might ask *that* question is the last thing you need.

So take a few moments to prepare and commit to memory an answer to the question(s) you're dreading. So if an interviewer does ask 'Why exactly did you leave your last job?' (and you were fired) or 'You haven't mentioned what degree class you got – what did you get in the end?' (when you didn't finish university), you have an answer at the ready.

In putting your response together, consider that you want to state your case in no more than a couple of sentences. You want to answer the question but then move on to make a positive comment about your commitment and enthusiasm for this particular job opportunity. Consider the following examples:

- 'I did have to take some time away from work because of ill-health. But I was given a clean bill of health and returned to full-time work nearly a year ago. I'm now very much focused on making the next step in my career.'

- 'I only worked at that company for six weeks because the role wasn't what I was expecting. However, that was early on in my career and I have definitely learned since then to do a lot more research and to ask in depth about the nature of the job.'

- 'I was made redundant from that job. But so were two other people in my department due to cost cuts that had to be made. But I can assure you that I'm raring to go and quite excited about the vacancy that we're talking about today.'

7 Ask clever questions to show that you're clever

Towards the end of an interview, most interviewers will ask: 'Do you have any questions for us?' And your answer should always be 'yes'. Saying that you have no questions is like saying that you're not really interested in the company. Answer 'no' and you may as well be saying 'No, because I'm not sufficiently bothered by the job to want to find out anything else about it.'

Avoid asking questions about holiday entitlement, the pay package, or whether you might need to do overtime. No matter how you phrase it, those sorts of questions could be interpreted by the interviewers as evidence that you're a slacker, more interested in what you can get out of the company than what you're willing to put in.

So prepare some good questions, for example on topics such as:

- The nature of the work itself, e.g. 'Of course I've read the job description, but could you tell me a little more about what I'd be doing on a day-to-day basis please?' or 'How would my performance be measured?'

- Training and development opportunities, e.g. 'What kind of training might I be able to get in the role?' or, if appropriate, 'Once I've done this job for a few years, what kinds of opportunities might this lead to?'

- The culture of the team and organisation, e.g. 'How would you describe the culture of the firm?' or 'I've read about the company on the website, but could you tell me a little bit about your reasons for choosing to work here please?'

8 Plan with military precision

If you're prone to worrying, don't let the logistics of the day let you down. Plan for your interview as if you were planning for a military campaign. Figure out:

- **What you are going to wear.** Have your suit cleaned and pressed. Get a haircut the week before so you look smart. If you aren't sure about the dress code – business suit or smart casual? – phone ahead. And, for specific advice on what to wear, consider asking friends for help (see 'Take Action: Dressing for success' on pages 62–3).

- **Your route and journey times**. Aim to get there an hour early. If you're early, you can always kill time in a local café reading a newspaper. Better that than arriving late and in a panic.

- **Exactly who is interviewing you**. Find out the number of interviewers, plus their names and job titles. That way, you won't have to worry about forgetting or mispronouncing a difficult name when you are introduced to your interviewers.

- **What written information is available about the job and the organisation**. Ask for a job description, the organisation's website address, and any brochures. That way you won't ask questions during the interview that you should have known the answers to.

9 Manage your emotions

I've covered a lot of techniques and exercises in Part 1 that you can use to feel more confident and in control. But here are three of the most powerful ones that you can use specifically for interviews.

- Use **visualisation** to run through how you would like the interview to go (see 'Confidence Booster: Using the movie screen in your head' on pages 48–9). See yourself shaking hands with the interviewers, giving them a confident smile. See yourself making good eye contact; imagine the questions they ask and the confident answers that you give while displaying open and confident body language.

- To boost your confidence on the big day, **create a folio of your achievements** (see 'Take Action: Considering the FACTs of life' on pages 122–3).

- In the moments before the interview, perhaps while you're waiting in reception, use either **diaphragmatic breathing** or the **ABCD technique** to defuse negative emotions (see 'Confidence Booster: Diaphragmatic breathing' on page 55 and 'Confidence Booster: Calming your emotions with ABCD' on pages 56–7).

10 Present your best self

Interviewers want to hire people who are skilled *and* friendly. They'd rather not appoint a skilled but unfriendly person. So interviewers are as strongly influenced by how you come across as by what you say.

Some experts reckon that you should 'be yourself' during an interview. But I suggest that you instead present your 'best self'. You probably don't behave the same way in front of your boss as in front of your team mates, your friends, or your grandparents. So it makes sense to present your most professional and friendly face during an interview.

Think about your body language and tone of voice (see also Chapter 3). Use your gestures, posture, and appropriate smiles. Make sure you *sound* interested and as if you had a great time when you're talking about your achievements. If you're in any doubt as to how you come across, make a recording of yourself during a mock interview with a friend and watch it back.

Especially during the first few minutes of the interview, focus on both *what* you say and *how* you say it. There's a lot of truth in the observation that many interviewers make their minds up within the first minutes of an interview. First impressions *do* count. Make them count for you.

13

Confident life change

CONFIDENCE

Making changes in our lives can be daunting. Quitting a job, taking a new one, moving house, entering into a new relationship, leaving a bad situation, deciding to start a business or a family, kicking a vice – the list goes on.

Human nature is inherently risk averse. We don't like the unknown so we worry about the challenges that change may throw up. Or we start to wonder if our current situation isn't quite as bad as we first thought. We may want to wait for the 'right time', which of course may never come around. No wonder we sometimes end up doing nothing and sticking with the status quo.

If you need to make a speedy and specific change in one area of your life right now, this chapter is for you. The last 20 years have seen a surge in research on how to bring about personal change. So I can share with you the hard science behind 10 essential steps to making change happen.

1 Give it some hard thought

You might know people who tell you to 'just do it', to go ahead and make the change. But rashly flinging yourself headlong into a new situation is rarely the best way to make change stick. Research backs up what you probably already knew anyway – that you're most likely to succeed at change by thinking it over and planning for it.

Scientists James Prochaska and Carlo DiClemente call this period of thinking *contemplation*, which is merely an elaborate word for thinking about the change from different angles. Their research shows that more contemplation is linked to more successful changes – and here are a couple of exercises to help you do it.

To kick off, start by weighing up the pros and cons of making the change. *Write out* – rather than just thinking through in your head – your answers to four questions:

- What are the benefits or advantages of making the change?
- What are the benefits of sticking with the status quo?
- What are the disadvantages or costs of making the change?
- What are the disadvantages of staying the same?

Once you've identified the pros and cons of your two alternatives, you can identify the actions you could take to make the change. Again by writing down your thoughts, work through these next questions:

- What could you do to maximise the benefits of making the change?
- What could you do to minimise the costs or disadvantages of making the change?

2 Consider your life from a different point of view

One of the best ways of working out what you should do is to imagine what someone else might say about your situation.

Imagine you are your own best friend. What observations and advice would you offer up about your situation? Have a think and write yourself a letter describing your dilemma and possible solutions (see 'Confidence Booster: Corresponding with your inner coach' on pages 147–8). Don't worry if you aren't sure what to say. Just start writing or typing. The beauty of the letter-writing technique is that words and ideas somehow tumble freely from your subconscious mind.

3 Decide on what you want

Research also tells us that people are most successful at making lasting changes happen in their lives when they pursue desirable goals rather than merely trying to run away from bad situations.

So take a little time to think about what you'd like to have in your life.

Chapter 4 has plenty of advice on goals. But focus on the sections 'Peering into the crystal ball' and 'Crafting a confident future'. Then create your vision of how you would like your life to look in the future (see 'Take Action: Creating your vision' on pages 80–1). Most people find that having at least a sense of how they would like their futures to look can keep them motivated through the tricky moments of bringing about personal change. Remember to use positive language in creating your vision; make an effort to focus on what you want your life to look like rather than simply writing about what you're trying to get away from.

4 Talk it through

The poet John Donne once wrote: 'No man is an island.' Of course, no woman is an island either. And there's no reason you need to struggle with your situation on your own.

So turn to your friends. Tell them what's going on and what you're thinking about doing. The simple act of articulating what's going on inside our heads can often help us to realise what we need to do.

And friends often have valuable advice and different perspectives. They may surprise you with some of their ideas. For example, they may suggest options that you hadn't thought about before. A great way to identify who may be best for supporting you during this period of change is to audit your friends (see 'Take Action: Choosing your comrades with care' on pages 118–20).

In your darkest moments, you may feel you have no one to turn to. But human beings are innately social and empathetic.

Whether in person, by email, telephone, or instant messenger, you may be surprised by how willing people are to get involved. So talk to the people around you, tell them what's going on with you and see what you can come up with together.

5 Get started sooner rather than later

Even big life decisions can usually be broken down into a number of smaller actions. If you're starting a new job, you may need to buy a new outfit, figure out your new route to work, find out more about the company, meet your boss, and so on. If you're splitting up with an unsatisfactory partner, you may need to put money aside, divide up your belongings, find a new place to live, get the post redirected.

So start getting those actions down on paper. To begin with, don't worry about which ones to do first or exactly how you will accomplish them. Just create one long list of every action – big and small. Change often feels most daunting when it is intangible and unspecific. But break down a big change into its smaller parts and you will see that they can be managed.

Next, turn your list of actions into an action plan (see the section 'Building momentum' in Chapter 4). Think about what you will do, who else might be involved, where and when you will do each one. Keep breaking down big goals until they feel like bite-sized actions that you could take on, one at a time.

6 Ride out the emotional rollercoaster

Another key research finding is that people are more likely to stick with a change when they understand the ups and downs that they will experience. Making change is not an overnight process. Even if you make the change overnight – say by telling your boss that you quit or by putting the deposit down on a new house – your emotions may still feel as if they are stuck in the past.

It's entirely normal to feel ambivalent, confused, uncertain, or even downright terrified. When you take on a new challenge, you can feel as if you have taken one step forward only to take two steps back (see also the section 'Good days and bad' in Chapter 7). You may make mistakes or occasionally lapse into old, bad habits. Some days you may feel that you've made a terrible blunder or that you no longer have the energy to carry on with your plan at all.

So keep reminding yourself that change is rarely an easy ride. And that confidence is all about doing what we need to do to help us attain our longer-term goals, even if it feels temporarily a bit nerve-wracking or uncomfortable in the present (see also the section 'Confidence is about action' in Chapter 1).

Plus you can help yourself survive the bumpy ride by assembling a first aid kit of resources. Before you embark on your big change, consider how to make yourself feel better when you feel down (see 'Take Action: Tapping your reserves of confidence' on page 114). Like a first aid kit for treating physical injuries, you should have one on hand in case of psychological emergencies. You don't wait until you're bleeding from a bad cut before you go buy one!

7 Take that first step

Making a personal change can feel like doing a parachute jump. Once you take that first step, the rest happens pretty much of its own accord. But we may struggle to take that first step.

Remember that circumstances rarely change of their own accord. By not choosing to take action, you are conspiring with yourself to remain unhappy. *You* are the only person who can dig yourself out of your situation.

The rut-busting Confidence Booster (on page 109) can be a handy way to take that first step. Look over your list of actions and choose a fairly straightforward one that you could do today. If you want to get fit, go for a brisk walk – you don't have to stump up the cash to join the gym. If you want to quit smoking, maybe hold off on the first cigarette of the day until after lunch if you can't quite bear to give up entirely yet.

Write down the advantages of taking that first small step and the disadvantages of doing nothing. Write down the excuses or reasons you are using to justify doing nothing – you'll be able to see them for what they're worth once you've committed them to paper. And finally, work out how you could reward yourself to celebrate taking that first step. Just one small action to begin with – you can do it!

8 Keep moving

Making a successful change is more often about taking regular, small steps than trying to make great leaps all at once. Aim to do too much in one go and you set yourself up to fail.

At times you may feel that small steps aren't moving you forward fast enough. But all successful human endeavours have been created over a period of time. Say you're starting a course of study, accept that you may at first find it difficult to concentrate. If you've moved in with someone new, allow yourself time to get used to your new setup.

What's more important than the speed of change is to keep going in the right direction. A gritty resolve to keep going, day by day, delivers results. Like the tortoise and the hare, slow and steady beats fast but erratic every time.

9 Set a daily goal

To keep yourself moving forward, aim to do something to move your life forwards every single day. Towards the end of the day, perhaps after you've finished work or are preparing for bed, plan out the actions (or even just one single action) that you will do the next day to keep your momentum going. For example, if you're aiming to find a new job, you might plan to spend 20 minutes at lunchtime flicking through the newspapers to look for relevant vacancies. If you're looking to move on from a relationship breakdown, you might set yourself a goal of calling eight estate agents to see if you can find a new place to live in.

The next day, do whatever you promised yourself you would do. And then set a new goal for the day after that.

I've said it before but shall say it again: remember that change takes time. Olympic athletes take years to get into peak physical and mental condition. People take months to find new jobs, move on from bad relationships and into better ones, lose weight, and so on. But if you're doing something every day, you will keep making progress and ensure that you stay on track. So what could *you* do tomorrow?

10 Celebrate your wins

To keep your motivation high, make sure you celebrate your successes. Find a way to congratulate yourself that works for you. Buy yourself a treat or gift if you feel you deserve it. Even if you don't want to spend money, at least note your achievement and give yourself the recognition you deserve (see 'Confidence Booster: Putting the icing on the confidence cake' on pages 166–7).

People often feel that the achievement of a goal should be its own reward. But that's not how the human brain works.

The more you celebrate and make a big deal of what you have achieved, the more confident you will feel about your ability to achieve even more.

Handling conflict with confidence

Hardly anyone enjoys conflict, but of course life is full of it. We get into everything ranging from minor disagreements over who should do which household chores to outright arguments over our work, finances, relationships and so on.

When we are faced with conflict, we often don't handle it well. We know that we need to be assertive. But many of us end up either backing down too quickly (being too passive) or getting too pushy or angry (being too aggressive). In this chapter, I present 10 tips for finding the perfect middle ground between being too passive and too aggressive. You will learn to stand up for your rights in an assertive manner and handle conflict with confidence.

1 Recognise that you have rights

Perhaps you're the one who ends up doing all of the housework. Or a colleague is shirking their workload and dumping it all on you. Maybe you're not happy with the state of your relationship or you want to speak up about someone's inappropriate or hurtful behaviour. Whatever the situation, you probably feel torn: part of you feels annoyed but another big part of you doesn't want to have to raise the issue.

The first step is to realise that you have a right to tell people how you feel. That doesn't necessarily mean that you will get everything you might wish for. But remember that other people aren't telepathic. They can't read your thoughts and know what you want – unless you tell them. When you do speak up, you may find that people are actually quite reasonable and willing to make at least small changes to their behaviour. So resolve to say what's on your mind. Bear with me, I'll tell you how to make this as painless as possible.

2 Realise that it's rarely a case of right versus wrong

What's your favourite food? Perhaps it's chocolate, a big juicy steak, a piece of cake, or something more exotic. Thing is, I can guarantee that there are other people out there who hate whatever you love. The same goes for your favourite film, book, TV show, actor, piece of clothing, and holiday destination. Whatever you like, I bet that there are more than a few people out there who can't stand it!

The point is that we all have different tastes and points of view. Even when you and I are presented with exactly the same food, film, or whatever else, we may have completely different feelings about them. That doesn't mean that either of us is 'right' or 'wrong'. We simply have a difference of opinion.

And when it comes to conflict, a good starting point is to recognise that it is rarely a case of right versus wrong. No doubt *both* of you feel that you are right. You can both explain your actions and feel that you have good reasons for acting the way you do. So trying to convince people that you are right and they are wrong simply isn't going to work. Instead, reframe the situation and try to see it as a difference of opinion between yourself and them. If you can bear that in mind as you raise the issue, you will be much more likely to have a calm and constructive discussion rather than an argument.

3 Initiate the conversation with 'we' rather than 'you'

Remember that most disagreements come down to a difference of opinion rather than one person being right and the other person being wrong. Keeping that in mind, it's a good idea to avoid talking about what you think the other person is or isn't doing.

For example, you may feel that I'm lazy and not doing my fair share of the household chores. But I may feel that I work hard all day and that life is too short to spend any more time than is strictly necessary cleaning up around the house. If you say 'You're not doing enough work around the house', it immediately puts me on the defensive. It implies that you're right and I'm wrong.

In fact, using the word 'you' can often sound more like an accusation than a statement. So avoid starting any sentences with the word 'you' at all.

Instead, remember that you and the other person are simply experiencing a difference of opinion. Try talking about the two of you by using the word 'we'. For example, you could broach the issue by saying: 'We seem to have different ideas when it comes to sharing the household chores. Can we talk about it please?'

Doesn't that sound a lot less confrontational?

4 Talk about your feelings

We're often taught that we should be rational, objective people and that we shouldn't let our emotions cloud our judgement. But the truth is that we often have very strong feelings – we're human, not robots! Pretending not to have feelings by refusing to discuss them can actually make a conversation *more* rather than less difficult.

One good reason for mentioning your feelings is that you let the other person know about the strength of your feeling about the issue. Another good reason is that your feelings can't be disputed. Sure, the other person could go on the offensive and argue about the alleged facts of the situation. But if you say 'I felt really upset when I thought you talked over me the other day' or 'I feel angry because I get the impression that you don't care enough about me to make an effort', no one can dispute how you feel.

I'm not saying that you should talk endlessly about your feelings or let all of your emotions come pouring out. However, after you're broached the discussion, a good way to get your point of view across is to talk about how you feel. So what will you say? 'I felt ...' or 'I feel ...' – what did or do you feel exactly?

5 Explain that you'd like to work together on resolving the issue

If you go into a conversation hoping to change someone's mind or 'prove' that the other person is wrong, you will almost certainly be disappointed. The best way of entering into any difficult conversation is by explaining that you're trying to understand what happened and figure out *together* a way forward.

Say something like: 'Let me be clear that I'm not trying to blame you for what happened. What I'd like to do is hear your point of view to make sure that I'm not jumping to conclusions. Then I'd like to tell you what I think happened. Then could we talk about how to resolve the situation please?'

Here's another example: 'From my point of view, I feel that you're being inconsiderate. I realise that I only have part of the picture and it doesn't take into account your point of view. So could you help me to put things into perspective by telling me what you think is going on please?'

By using this kind of language, you're making it clear that you're not trying to blame anyone. You recognise that you know only part of what happened and can't possibly know the whole story. And you're inviting the other person to be a full participant in the conversation. You're not simply bashing them over the head with what you think they are doing wrong and how you think they should change their behaviour.

6 Give the other person the opportunity to talk

Once you've extended the invitation and said that you would like to hear their side of the story, you will find that most people are more than ready to talk. The challenge here is to ensure that you listen, that you give the other person the full weight of your attention without interrupting.

To make sure you understand the other person's point of view completely, you may wish to use gentle prompts such as:

- ■ 'How do you see what's happened?'
- ■ 'How are you feeling about this?'
- ■ 'Tell me more about why this is important to you.'
- ■ 'Can you tell me why you think we've ended up like this?'

As you ask your questions, you may find that the other person makes some comments that seem wholly unjustified, totally wrong. But you need to avoid responding at this point. Your aim should only be to ask questions and listen.

A lot of the time, people get into arguments because they feel that the other person isn't truly listening. If you can stay quiet and let the other person talk, you will be much more likely to have a productive conversation. If you interrupt and try to explain your point of view or justify what you did or didn't do, then the volume of the conversation will almost certainly escalate; both of you will get louder and louder until it simply becomes a shouting match.

7 *Demonstrate* that you are listening

Listening isn't a totally passive affair though. Your active participation is required too; your role is to acknowledge what's being said. You need to acknowledge the feelings that are being expressed. Even if you don't agree with the points or concerns that the other person is raising, you can still show that you understand the importance of their feelings.

So if someone says 'I was so angry', try paraphrasing what you're hearing by saying 'I didn't realise it then, but I appreciate *now* that you were really angry.' If someone says 'You don't seem to understand the pressure that I'm under', say 'I didn't understand that you felt that way, but now I do.'

Remember that we're only human. Even though we might try to pretend that we don't have feelings or attempt to push them away, it's actually only when we acknowledge how other people are feeling that we can get to the heart of the matter. Especially if you notice that the other person is repeating the same message over and over again, take it as a sign that you need to paraphrase more.

8 Say what you mean

Only when the other person has finished speaking should you try to get across your side of the story. Bear in mind that people aren't mind readers. If you feel disappointed or angry or frustrated, you have to tell people how you feel – you can't expect them to read between the lines and guess what's really on your mind!

So avoid skirting around the issue. Recall that by now you've given the other person plenty of opportunity to talk about the situation. So be straight. Avoid saying only part of what you want to say in the hopes that the other person will be able to intuit the rest – because that just won't happen.

Remember that you only have part of the overall story. So make sure you use phrases such as 'I feel that you ...' rather than just saying 'You ...' Or if you have an opinion to give, make it clear that it is only your personal viewpoint by saying 'My feeling is that ...' or 'I believe that ...'

When you've finished speaking, check that the other person has really heard and understood what you had to say. Perhaps ask: 'I know I've said a lot and it may be a lot to take on board. Would you mind telling me what you think I've just been saying so far please?'

9 Work together on finding a solution

Say a friend broke your treasured ornament, your partner dented the car, or a colleague let you down. Thing is: you can't change the past. Whatever happened has happened. The only thing we can ever do is to look for ways of moving forward, of either resolving the situation in the present or putting steps in place to make sure that it won't happen again in the future.

So say that. Extend the invitation to the other person: 'Well now that we've discussed what seems to have happened, what can we do to move on?'

If you've given people enough opportunity to talk (and shown them that you understand their point of view), you will almost certainly find that they are by now much more amenable to having a rational discussion about what to do next. If you do find the conversation begins to get heated again, go back to steps 6 and 7. Ask more questions and acknowledge the feelings that get aired. Only then can you continue to have a productive conversation and hopefully find a way to resolve your conflict.

10 Press pause

Of course you may not always be the one initiating the conversation. On occasion, other people may come to you saying that they want to tell you about something you did that was wrong or felt inappropriate to them. If that happens, simply listen to what they have to say.

Let the other person talk and talk and talk. Let them speak until they have finished whatever they have to say. Avoid interrupting. Don't try to defend your actions or explain there and then. Do ask questions if anything isn't clear. Otherwise, simply listen and allow them to get whatever they have to say off their chest.

Only when they're finished, say something like 'Thank you for sharing that with me. That's a lot to take on board and I'd like to think about it before I respond.' You might also say 'That's a real surprise to me because I had no idea you felt that way.' Then set up a second meeting – it could be later on the same day or several days later if it's a major issue that you need to do a *lot* of thinking about. That buys you enough time to work through what you want to say, by going back to the very beginning of this chapter.

15

Health, fitness and body confidence

Many people would like to be healthier, fitter and more confident about their bodies. Perhaps you're working long hours and eating too much (or too much of the wrong stuff). You may be trying to smoke less or drink less. Or perhaps you want to shed a little weight or get fitter so you feel happier with how you look. The good news is that it's never too late to start.

When I was studying for my undergraduate degree in psychology, I worked as a gym instructor at the University of Bristol. When I did my Ph.D. in psychology, I taught hundreds of exercise classes for people of all ages, shapes and sizes too. So if you'd like to get healthier and feel more positive about your body, put your trust in me and read on.

1 Have realistic expectations

Perhaps you want to eat more healthily, drink less alcohol or have more energy. Maybe you want to tone up, lose weight or gain muscle. Maybe you're a woman who wants to reduce certain 'problem' body parts or a man who wants bigger arms. Whatever your goals, remember that success will come with time. Changing your habits and body takes months.

Many people feel disappointed that they aren't changing quickly enough. In particular, people trying to lose weight feel that they aren't making any progress. But many of the changes may be subtle and undetectable. For example, people who begin to exercise may lose fat but gain muscle instead – they may stay the same weight or even put on a little weight. However, the good news is that they will be losing inches all over their bodies, around their waists and hips and thighs. So if you're trying to improve your health, fitness and body confidence, remember that change takes time.

2 Start today with micro-goals

Listen to most gym instructors and they'll tell you that you need to engage in a certain number of minutes of exercise at a certain intensity for a particular number of times every week. Yes, that's *one* way of shaping up – but certainly not the only way. So ignore them and listen to me instead.

Research shows that you don't have to spend hours in a gym to lose weight and restore your body confidence. You can ease yourself more gently into a healthier lifestyle by setting micro-goals for yourself such as:

- walking up a flight of stairs at work
- getting away from your desk at lunchtime to go for a brisk 10-minute walk
- playing Frisbee on a Sunday afternoon
- dancing around your bedroom to your favourite upbeat song
- replacing your afternoon chocolate bar with a pot of fruit salad bought from the supermarket
- walking around a museum or gallery one evening every couple of weeks
- doing just 10 press-ups or sit-ups during the ad break of your favourite TV show
- getting off the bus one stop earlier and walking the rest of the way.

Every little counts. It all adds up. Our bodies evolved to be able to burn energy even in very short bursts. So it may not seem all that much to decide to walk up a flight of stairs. But if you do it once a day for the first week, then twice a day the next week, then three times a day the week after that, it will all make a difference. Gradually increase the number of micro-goals you set yourself. After a few months, you may be surprised at how big a difference it's making.

If you'd like to work on other aspects of your health, take a gradual approach too. For example, consider micro-goals such as:

- Cutting out one coffee a day and replacing it with a glass of water – just one cup a day shouldn't be too difficult to begin with, right?

- Not smoking for a couple of hours a day, for example between 10 a.m. and 1 p.m. if you usually pop out for a mid-morning cigarette

- Replacing every third alcoholic drink with a non-alcoholic one to begin the process of cutting down a little. After doing that for a few weeks, you could try to replace every other alcoholic drink. Or buy a non-alcoholic drink for yourself every time it's your turn to pay.

So what micro-goals could *you* commit to starting right away?

3 Eat more vegetables and eat for health

Whatever your specific goals, you can't really go wrong if you aim to eat more vegetables. Rather than thinking about having to diet and give up or restrict certain foods, adopt the mindset that you are simply going to *add* more vegetables, pulses and salads, and some fruit to your intake. The British government suggests that we should eat five portions of fruit and vegetables every day. One portion is about as much as you'd be able to hold in a cupped hand. So an apple, a banana or a mango counts as one portion of fruit. Several spoonfuls of peas, broccoli, or carrots count as a portion too.

Just a couple of portions of fruit is enough for most people. But with vegetables, you can't really go wrong. Vegetables are lower in sugar than fruits and contain fibre, which helps our bodies to get rid of toxins more quickly. They are low in calories but fill us up quickly so we feel fuller for longer and less tempted to snack on unhealthy foods. Neither can you overdose on them. Other countries suggest that their citizens eat up to seven or even nine portions of fruit and vegetables a day – there are no harmful effects of having too many vegetables.

When it comes to other foodstuffs, choose food that is healthy rather than food that is aimed at controlling your weight or calorie intake. For example, the label on a bag of crisps may claim that it's 'lower fat' or only so many calories. But deep-down you probably know that it's never really going to be a healthy food, right?

4 Strengthen your resolve through social support

Research shows that we tend to pick up on the habits and attitudes (both good and bad) of the people around us. For example, studies show that the mere fact of knowing criminals makes people more likely to commit crimes and get caught for them too. Even obesity is catching – research shows that the more clinically obese people we know, the greater our own chances of succumbing.

So find ways to spend more time with people who have done what you want to achieve. If you're looking to quit smoking, try to spend a little more time with your non-smoking friends. If you're looking to shed the pounds, hang out with a few more people who've done the same.

Be careful of friends who may be holding you back. They may say 'No, you don't need to change' or 'You're already perfect as you are', but often that says more about their state of happiness (or unhappiness) about themselves rather than what they feel is genuinely in your best interests. They may feel threatened by the changes you're trying to make and be trying to hold you back to make themselves feel better. Make an effort to identify supportive friends who are open-minded about the new, better life you are trying to carve out for yourself. If you're serious about making changes to your health, fitness and body confidence, see also the section 'Frenemies and friends' in Chapter 5.

Finally, share your goals with all of your good friends, the people who genuinely care about you. Psychologists have discovered that we try to behave in ways that are consistent with what we tell other people. So if you tell people about your goals, you will be more likely to achieve them. If you say to your friends that you're going to lose weight or quit smoking, they can remind you of your commitments, chivvy you along, and support you when temptation may be calling.

5 Create a vision to sustain your motivation

In Chapter 4 I talk about the importance of having a vision. A vision is just an image of the life you'd like to be leading. It's a good idea to create a vision because it can help to buoy your motivation when you're tempted to quit. Take some time to write about what your future life will be like once you reach your health, fitness or body goals.

Research shows that people who set negative goals (e.g. 'I want to shift the fat off my stomach area') are less likely to succeed than people who set positive goals (e.g. 'I will be slim enough to fit into that elegant outfit that I saw'). So make sure your vision is filled with all of your upbeat thoughts about how you will feel, the activities you'll be able to do, the conversations you'll have with friends and the compliments you'll receive from them, and so on. The act of picturing your desired future *and writing about it* will help to reduce your chances of lapsing into bad habits.

However, remember that a vision is just a motivational tool. It's your *action* (and not the vision alone) that will allow you to achieve your goals. So make sure you take action, actual steps, perhaps even micro-goals that allow you to move towards your goals.

6 Guard against your future impulses

No matter how good our intentions, we all lack willpower at times. Like many people, I know that if I have bags of crisps or chocolate in the house, I'll end up eating them. So one of the ways in which we can help ourselves to avoid eating unhealthy snacks is by not buying them at the supermarket.

Clear out your cupboards of unhealthy foods. Don't just put them at the back of the cupboard – that's still too easy for you to get to. Go to the supermarket after you've had a decent meal so you feel full and less tempted by unhealthy snacks so that you can stock up on healthier foods. Plan what you would like to cook over the next few days and make a list – that'll help you to eat well and feel full on healthier foods. Plus, when you are at home and feeling tempted, at least you won't have anything unhealthy on hand.

Of course, the same goes for cigarettes or alcohol if that's what you're trying to cut back on or avoid. And if you're trying to do more exercise, find a friend that you can buddy up with. Making an arrangement or having a commitment to do an activity with a friend makes you far more likely to go through with it because no one likes to let other people down.

7 Concentrate on what you're putting into your body

A lot of us eat and drink too much because we're only dimly aware of what we're doing. A lot of us eat while we're in front of the television. Or we may drink too much because we're with friends and enthralled by the conversation we're having. A great tip for cutting back is to eat and drink only when we can concentrate fully (this tip is related to the notion of mindfulness – see the section 'Focusing on the here and now' in Chapter 5).

Whenever you want to eat, turn off the television. Whatever you're eating, really concentrate on what you're putting into your mouth. Whether you feel a craving for a chocolate bar or a healthy snack, eat it slowly. Avoid grabbing any food on the go and eating it on the move. Sit down and make the food your sole focus. Imagine that you've never had the food before and want to savour it properly. Chew your food slowly, notice the aroma of your food, think about the texture, and experience the different tastes. Of course we want to eat with our families, but eating alone occasionally can help us to re-learn how to appreciate our food properly, which helps us to eat less.

The same goes if you want to have an alcoholic drink. Avoid doing it in a crowded bar or at a party with friends when the alcohol isn't your primary focus. Sip your drink, savour it. Taste the alcohol, feel the sensations if creates within you.

Slow down when you eat and drink. Once you decide to do these activities only when you can concentrate on them intently, you will find that you naturally eat and drink less.

8 Watch what you watch and read

Several research studies suggest that what we watch on television and see in magazines can affect our attitudes towards ourselves and our bodies. Julie Albright, a professor of psychology at the University of Southern California, completed a study showing that women who watched TV shows about plastic surgery were more anxious about their bodies. So avoid watching them entirely.

Similar studies have found that both women and men who are presented with glossy images of people with perfect bodies feel worse about themselves too. Whether you're reading *Vogue* or *Men's Health*, remember that the models have spent hours in make-up, have been dressed by top stylists and lit and photographed by world-class photographers. On top of that, they've been air-brushed too, perhaps lengthening their legs, ironing out wrinkles, making women's breasts bigger and eyelashes longer. They even make men's biceps bigger and jaws squarer too. So cut down on how much you read glossy magazines and you will allow yourself to set more realistic expectations for yourself and your body.

9 Celebrate your progress with experiences

Psychologists know that the best way to change someone's behaviour is by rewarding the desired behaviour. Punishment isn't terribly effective. So avoid beating yourself up and by all means celebrate your progress.

So what could you do to celebrate your health and body confidence milestones? Perhaps buy yourself a CD, a new gadget you had your eye on, or an item of clothing. Get tickets to the cinema or arrange to have a fun evening with a good friend. Definitely do celebrate, but I'd recommend that you avoid celebrating by rewarding yourself with food, drink, or whatever else you're trying to cut down on.

Say you're trying to lose weight. By rewarding yourself with a piece of chocolate cake, you are subconsciously reinforcing the view that chocolate cake is desirable yet off-limits. You send your brain mixed messages by denying yourself certain foods most of the time and then gobbling them down at other times. So reward yourself with experiences and gifts rather than food and drink.

10 Review your progress from the point of view of your best friend

In an ideal world, we would make progress every single day and ever single week without ever slipping or faltering. But the reality is that we're all too human. Particularly when we're stressed or tired, we may give into temptation, perhaps foregoing a day at the gym, having a cigarette, having an unhealthy snack, or whatever else we shouldn't be doing.

When that happens, some people beat themselves up and fall into the trap of saying 'I'm a failure', 'I've failed' or 'I've blown it'. But try looking at it differently. If you told your best friend that you'd been too lazy to do any exercise one day, had a few cigarettes at the pub, or had a burger and fries one evening, what would he or she say? Good friends don't say things like 'You're a failure', 'You'll never succeed in your goals' or 'You've blown your diet now and should just give up'. So avoid criticising yourself too severely either.

Instead, look at your lapse as just a momentary stumble rather than a permanent failure. Some researchers suggest that lapses and stumbles may even be beneficial, helping our mind to come up with new tactics and strategies as it tries to correct what happened. Rather than counting the number of times you let yourself down, count the number of times you succeeded. If you had a healthy lunch and a healthy dinner on most days of the week but then pigged out on a Friday night, count the number of healthy lunches and dinners you had.

Keep asking yourself: 'What would my best friend say about this momentary lapse in the context of my ongoing success?' You'd probably hear good friends tell you messages like 'Remember that you still did fantastically well the rest of the week' or 'Don't worry about it! You kept with your diet for nearly six days so Friday night wasn't a big deal.'

Guilt and shame aren't healthy emotions. What's done is done. You can't turn back time and change what you did. All you can do is concentrate on what you will do from now on. Keep looking forwards, never back. Do that and you will continue to make good progress.

Quick confidence

The first seven chapters of this book are designed to guide you through a complete programme that will boost your confidence and allow you to make progress every day towards achieving your goals in life. I strongly recommend that you work through those chapters to achieve real, lasting change in your life. But sometimes you may need a quick boost of confidence in a hurry; you have hours and minutes to prepare for a stressful event rather than weeks or days.

So here are 10 of the fastest techniques I've found for calming negative feelings and lifting your confidence. Some of these are explained in more depth elsewhere in this book, and some are entirely new. But using just one or two of these should be enough if you're in a tight spot.

1 Write about your values

Research psychologists have investigated all sorts of methods to help people feel better about themselves. One successful intervention involves writing about your personal values. So the next time you want an extra injection of resolve, try this on for size.

Spend at least five minutes putting pen to paper to write about your personal values, what's important to you. Don't worry about grammar, spelling, or trying to complete full sentences. Just bring to mind the people that are most important to you, the goals that you want to achieve, and the reasons you want to achieve them. Concentrate intently on this task for around 10 minutes if you can.

Then, just as you get near to wrapping up, spend an extra minute or two writing about how your actions today are linked to your values and goals. Do that and you will steel yourself for whatever you need to do right now.

2 Inhale, exhale, inhale, and exhale

Diaphragmatic breathing is one of the simplest ways to restore your emotional centre (see 'Confidence Booster: Diaphragmatic breathing' on page 55). Take slow, deep breaths into your belly and then let them out again.

The key here is to focus on your breathing and nothing else. Anxious thoughts may still drift into your mind – it happens to most people. But your goal is to avoid engaging with those thoughts. Simply bring your attention back to your breathing.

If you can, find somewhere quiet where you can focus on breathing slowly and deeply for five to ten minutes. Go get a coffee and sit by yourself. Find an empty room, lock yourself in a toilet cubicle, or even find a quiet spot in a café. Perhaps put your iPod earphones in and pretend you're listening to music if you don't want people to interrupt you. On the other hand, it doesn't matter too much if you're surrounded by people. You may hear snatches of their conversations, but just keep bringing your attention back to your breathing. Close your eyes if it helps you to focus on your breathing. Bring your awareness fully to your breathing and you will almost certainly find that you feel calmer, more centred, and more able to deal with whatever life may have to throw at you.

3 Sing and dance

Figure out what your favourite upbeat song is. It should be something up-tempo that you probably already know most of the words to. Put it on your iPod, burn it onto a CD, or do whatever works for you so you have it to hand when you might next need a shot of confidence.

Then, when you need to lift your mood, get your song out and listen to it. If you're alone and no one can hear you, then sing along to it too. Dance and let your body go wild. Physical exercise (see tip 6 later in this chapter) may release feel-good chemicals called endorphins into your body, so that's why I suggest waving your arms around, swinging your hips, and letting yourself go to your favourite song. If you work in an open plan office, perhaps go hide in a toilet cubicle with your iPod and at least shake your head and point your fingers to the beat.

Sing, dance, clap and stamp your feet. You'll find it very difficult to feel low after you've listened to the whole of your favourite song. This technique has worked for everyone I know who's every tried it. Give it a go!

4 Be your own personal trainer, coach and cheerleader

'You can do it!' While completing my Ph.D. in psychology, I used to work as a personal trainer and I currently work as an executive coach. And much of what I do is simply to offer encouragement. The good news is that research shows that you can be your own personal trainer and coach too.

Whatever your situation, imagine that you have a personal trainer/coach/cheerleader urging you on. What would he or she say? If you can, take a few minutes to write down a half-dozen sentences to get you motivated (see 'Confidence Booster: Creating your cool CATs' on page 31). Even if you don't have pen and paper handy, you can bring to mind your own inner coach and imagine him or her shouting out those words of support. Really hear those words of encouragement!

This technique is probably my personal favourite. I use it before I'm due to give a big presentation. I use it when I'm at the gym and need just a little bit of a boost to get me through the end of my workout. I do it when I'm struggling with a problem and can't see the answer. Why don't you give it a go yourself?

5 Focus on the positives

Take a sheet of paper and write the numbers 1 to 20 down the side of the page. Then write down 20 positive comments about yourself. For example, you could write down characteristics about yourself that you're proud of or have ever been complimented on, such as your kindness or honesty, your flexibility or loyal nature, your caring nature or artistic streak.

You should also include any of your achievements and accomplishments in life. Think about achievements in the broadest sense of the word. Avoid limiting yourself purely to your work. If you have good friends, a loving partner, a close relationship with a sibling, and so on, remember that those are achievements too – many people don't have the relationships that you may sometimes take for granted.

If it's helpful, you could use the following sentence stems to prompt your thinking:

- I am …
- I have …
- I am grateful for …
- People can depend on me for …

Write down 20 positive comments about yourself and you help to banish unconstructive thoughts about yourself. In Chapters 4 and 5, I suggest exercises for listing both your strengths and achievements (see 'Take Action: Telling the story of your strengths' on pages 78–9 and 'Take Action: Considering the FACTs of life' on pages 122–3). I recommend that you do those exercises at some stage. If you do them, you can then flick back through what you wrote in those exercises to prompt yourself before scribbling down your list of 20 positive comments about yourself and your life.

6 Get physical

I completed a Ph.D. in sport and exercise psychology and one experiment I conducted with Professor David Hemsley at the Institute of Psychiatry looked at the effects of physical exercise on people's moods. Amazingly, we found that even one session of exercise not only quelled negative emotions such as anxiety and depression, but also boosted positive emotions such as joy and excitement.

If you think about it, a lot of the bad feelings we experience are associated with being quite still physically. We sit or stand still to cry, mope, worry, or feel sorry for ourselves. It's much tougher to feel down when you're jogging or jumping up and down on the spot!

If you want to lift your confidence and outlook on life, go put your trainers on. Go to the gym, have a jog, play football, do a yoga class, get on your bike.

But even if you can't get changed to do some sport or exercise, at least spend a few minutes raising your heart rate. Bounce up and down on the spot. Go for a brisk walk. Walk up and down a flight of stairs a few times. Spend as little as 10 minutes doing something to get your heart beating a bit faster and the research tells us that you will almost certainly feel better about yourself.

7 Have 10 minutes of 'worry time'

Sometimes your head may be filled with anxious thoughts. Perhaps you're replaying something awful that happened or you're worrying about what might happen or what could go wrong in the future. If that's ever the case, then pick up a sheet of paper and either two differently coloured pens or a pen and a highlighter. You're going to engage in 10 minutes of 'worry time'.

Start by setting a timer or taking note of the time: write it down at the top of your notepad so you don't lose track of time and spend too much time worrying.

Spend the next 10 minutes concentrating on all of your worries. Write down everything that you're concerned about. No one else will ever see this sheet of paper – you're going to tear it up afterwards – so write down every little detail, no matter how small or insignificant it might seem to other people. Get every worry down, all of your apprehensive thoughts and negative feelings.

Then stop. When your timer goes off or time is up, stop with the anxious thoughts. Now go back through what you've written and underline or highlight the issues that you can actually do something about. Write down at least three actions that you can take either now or in the next day or week. You should by now have exhausted your worries; if you find your mind drifting back to the same issues, remind yourself that you've already worried about them enough and done everything you can. In Chapter 5 (the 'Get ready to succeed' box on page 130), I talk about the difference between productive and unproductive worry. So worry time allows you to wallow (temporarily) in unproductive worry, while writing down the handful of practical actions allows you to rest assured that you will also take sensible steps to make sure you do whatever you can too.

8 Bring your emotions into check with ABCD

The ABCD technique (see 'Confidence Booster: Calming your emotions with ABCD' on pages 56–7) is one of the more powerful techniques for calming your emotions and freeing yourself of anxious thoughts. But it does require a little bit of practice, so expect to get the most benefit from it after you've used it a handful of times.

The four steps are described in Chapter 3. Remember that the beauty of the technique is that you're not trying to run away from your feelings, suppress them, or pretend that they don't exist. Our feelings are messages from our unconscious, so it's worth paying attention to them (briefly) by acknowledging 'I feel worried' or 'I'm so angry' or whatever else you may be feeling.

Once you've acknowledged how you're feeling, move your attention away from your feelings and onto your breathing. Take slow, deep breaths. Focus only on the rise and fall of your belly or perhaps the sound of air moving in and out of your nostrils as you breathe.

Then smile, chuckle quietly, or laugh out loud. You'll feel better for it. And then you'll be able to decide on what to do next.

9 Remind yourself that you are not your feelings

When we feel hurt, anxious, afraid or angry, our thoughts can rush around in our minds and we may act on autopilot. We may want to avoid a situation, lash out, or engage in any number of other inappropriate behaviours.

But as a psychologist, I help people to distinguish themselves from their thoughts and feelings. You have thoughts, but you are not your thoughts. You have feelings, but you are not your feelings. The essence of *you* is separate from your thoughts and feelings.

So if you're feeling worked up and want to feel more confident, try saying the following to yourself: 'I have thoughts, but I am not my thoughts. I have feelings but I am not my feelings. Confidence comes from taking action and I choose to take action. I can focus my mind on anything I want to and I choose to focus it on ...' and then add whatever task or goal you are trying to feel more confident about.

Read that paragraph, say it out loud and think about what it means. Help yourself to distance yourself from the negative thoughts and feelings that you may be experiencing.

10 Take a time out

There's a part of your brain called the amygdala that acts as your internal alarm system, alerting you that you need to pay attention to what's going on around you. When you are feeling overwhelmed, you can bet that your amygdala is going crazy. However, you can reset this unruly part of the brain and get it to calm down by performing an easy rote task.

For example, try doing one of these for five minutes:

- Take a sheet of paper and write about what your home looks like.

- Pick up a dictionary and copy out the meanings of 10 words you have never used before.

- Do some mental arithmetic. Start with the number 102 and subtract 6 from it until you get to zero. Then, if you still aren't feeling better, start with the number 104 and subtract 7 from it until you get to zero.

The key is to focus as intently as you can on the task. Sure, negative thoughts may still pop into your head. But you will find that they gradually have less and less of a hold over you.

And if you want to read more about the amygdala and how to keep it in check, do take a look at one of my other books: *Personality: How To Unleash Your Hidden Strengths* (also published by Prentice Hall Life). It has a chapter on emotional resilience as well as plenty of other advice and guidance for harnessing your personal assets and creating a successful life.

Index